FRANCIS DRAKE

IN THE

NEW WORLD

BY DONALD M. VILES

FRANCIS DRAKE IN THE NEW WORLD

DANCING MOON PRESS
NEWPORT, OREGON

Copyright © 2007 by Donna Sheldon

"Treasure Chests Of The Future" by Donald M. Viles was first published in *Lost Treasure*, April 1994, page 14. Reprinted by permission of *Lost Treasure* magazine.

ALL RIGHTS RESERVED.

No part of this book may be used or reproduced or transmitted in any form, or by any means, electronic or mechanical, including photocopy, recording, or any information storage and retrieval system, without written permission from the publisher, except in the case of brief quotations embedded in critical articles or reviews.

DANCING MOON PRESS
P.O. Box 832, Newport, OR 97365
541-574-7708
www.dancingmoonpress.com
carla@dancingmoonpress.com

Printed in the United States of America
Printed by LazerQuick of Newport, Oregon

Book design: Carla Perry

ISBN: 1-892076-24-1;
ISBN-13: 978-1-892076-24-3
Library of Congress Control Number: 2006930350
Viles, Donald M.
"Frances Drake In The New World"
Includes bibliographic references and index.
1. Title; 2. Francis Drake; 3. English History; 4. USA History;
5. Oregon State History; 6. New World Explorers;
7. Treasure hunting

FIRST EDITION

To Charlene

Whose patience with a
determined history-minded
husband made possible the
discovery of a true Northwest
American heritage.

Part I
Of this two-book series:

Frances Drake In The New World
by Donald M. Viles
ISBN-13: 978-1-892076-24-3

Part II
Of this two-book series

Hidden Heritage of New Spain
by Donald M. Viles and Charlene Viles
ISBN-13: 978-1-892076-25-0

both published by Dancing Moon Press
Newport, Oregon

MY FATHER, DONALD MARION VILES,

is the author of this book. While researching the history and geography of Francis Drake's track along the west coast of North America and then searching for the truth about Neah-Kah-Nie Mountain's mystery, he began writing for *Lost Treasure* magazine. The article that appears on the next few pages is our family's personal favorite.

My father put his heart and soul into the book you are about to read. I hope you enjoy reading it as much as he enjoyed writing it for you.

—Donna Viles Sheldon
2007

Terence Boone Jungling taken at Bar View, Oregon, August 1994

Treasure Chests Of The Future
by Donald M. Viles
first published in *Lost Treasure*, April 1994, page 14

For me there is yet to be the thrill and excitement of opening a treasure chest. I have found old Spanish mines that have been hidden for centuries, and solved an ancient archaeological mystery. These adventures, during the course of revealing their secrets, have made my body quiver with excitement. But to open a sealed treasure chest—that would be a supreme thrilling and nerve tingling electrification. The only way such an exciting experience could be of more heart-thumping anticipation would be to know such a chest existed, have it in sight, and know that it could not be opened until some time had passed.

My great-grandson (Terence Boone Jungling) was born just five weeks ago and I suddenly realized there was a new treasure adventure I can pass on, or be able to share if I am extremely lucky, to a time some years in the future.

Loaded treasure chests are difficult to find and most times hard to retrieve. Not only that, this type of treasure is not overly abundant. This, I realize, is something I can change.

Although not being the least bit clairvoyant, I can close my eyes and look into the future. Here I see a young man, maybe in his early teens, who can no longer stand the suspense. That treasure chest on the mantle has got to be opened. Who knows, maybe he can get Mom and Dad to open it, or maybe the suspense and curiosity will finally become overwhelming and someday he will decide to reveal its contents.

There will be a padlock on the chest, but the keys will be inside. To open it the first time will require taking the screws out of the hinges holding the lid. Perhaps it will take some planning to get a screwdriver and open it when Mom and Dad are not around. Then, of course, it will have to be put back together before the folks come back. It won't matter. The important thing is that "this is a treasure chest and treasure my great-grandfather made for me."

What do you put in a treasure chest for the future? Well, first of course, there must be coins. In this one there will be some U.S. Bicentennial coins; some Eisenhower Dollars; a Susan B. Anthony Dollar, and some "Wheat" pennies. Also included will be some Canadian coins. There will be some paper money that will include a Canada dollar and perhaps a U.S. Silver Certificate Dollar.

All treasure chests have jewels in them—everyone knows that. In this "pirate loot" I will include some semi-precious cut stones from India and China; a man's ring with a fire agate setting I made, and two ladies' rings—one with a stone I cut from a Thunder Egg, and one with a Citrine stone from China. Also included will be a string of semiprecious stone beads.

Before the treasure chest is closed for the last time (by me), it will have its lower section loaded with all the mentioned treasures plus enough U.S. coins to fill it. The top of the chest has a coin slot, so once closed there will still be room in the deep lid for lots of coins that will consist of my pocket change and any odd foreign coins I can scrounge.

Can't you just see a young man's eyes when he opens this treasure chest and the riches come pouring out to the floor? I can, and the odds are that I probably won't even be there. Like I said, it won't matter; he will always remember the treasure chest his great-grandfather made for him.

Maybe I should start another one. There might be a great-granddaughter some day. Hell, I might just make several.

Terence Boone Jungling with his sister Emilee Boone Jungling, in 2006. Taken by their father at Eagle Crest Resort in Oregon. Emilee was born thirteen months after her great-grandfather passed away.

CONTENTS

Treasure Chests of the Future viii
Prologue 13
Chapter 1 17
Chapter 2 29
Chapter 3 39
Chapter 4 43
Chapter 5 55
Chapter 6 58
Chapter 7 65
Chapter 8 78
Chapter 9 86
Chapter 10 94
Chapter 11 105

Postscript #1: Francis Drake Northwest 112
- Strait of Anian 116
- Drake's Bay 117
- Port New Albion 119
- Colnett's Map 119
- Island of California 120
- Rio Del Tizon 122
- Drake's Track 123

**Postscript #2: North America's Hidden Legacy
at Neah-Kah-Nie Mountain** 125
- The Mountain 125
- A Different Search 126
- Another Quest and Revelation 134
- Triangulation Survey by William Bourne 137
- Survey at Neah-Kah-Nie 139
- Francis Drake's Voyage 140

About the Author 148

Illustrations (Maps and Photographs)
Terence Boone Jungling, 1994 viii
Terence Boone Jungling & Emilee Boone Jungling x
Sir Francis Drake in 1586 16
Golden Hinde 16
Strait of Anian 117
Devil's Cove (Drake's Bay) 118
Hondius map and illustrations 119

CONTENTS (CONTINUED)

Illustrations (Maps and Photographs, continued)
James Colnett's map 120
New Mexico, Florida and Island of California 121
Island of California 122
Rio Del Tizon 123
Drake's Track – California to Arctic Circle 124
Treasure Rock (Figure 1) 127
Treasure Rock (Figure 2) 128
Augur Rock in 1969 129
Augur Rock Mark Explanation 130
Wendle's Rock 132
Wayne's Rock – Stone Triangle 133
Triangulation Survey by William Bourne 138
Survey at Neah-Kah-Nie 139
Queen Elizabeth I knighting Francis Drake 142
Donald M. Viles and Arline Viles 144
Freshman Class at Newport High School, 1935 145
Newport High School (building), 1935 145
Donald M. Viles self-portrait 146
Charlene Viles 147
Donald M. Viles unloading fishing boat 147
Donald M. Viles with printing press 149

Index 150

PROLOG

SIR FRANCIS DRAKE is freely conceded to be one of the greatest of all English seamen by world historians and many great mariners. Credited with masterminding the naval tactics that contributed considerably to the appalling devastation of the mighty fleet of great galleons in 1588—known historically as the Spanish Armada—and being the first known captain to navigate a vessel completely around the globe, Drake deserves to be immortalized.

Ferdinand Magellan is in the record books as being the original globe-circling mariner, but in truth he was not, for Magellan was killed before completing the complete track. It was the mate of his vessel *Victoria*, who completed the Magellan navigation.

Drake's around-the-world trek has been the subject of countless printed works, some of which romantically glorified him for "daring to singe the Spaniard's beard," in Spain's own pond, the Pacific Ocean. Other writers damned Drake intensely for being nothing more than a pirate who brazenly robbed gold bullion and silver plate from peaceful Spanish vessels whose only crime was minding their own business. But both foregoing opinions of Drake's actions while on his famous voyage are merely conjecture because of the deep mystery concerning this great feat.

Francis Drake, on the west coast of North America, has always been a puzzle to historians. There were some who did not believe the voyage was primarily one of piracy, either glorious or degrading.

In seventeenth century accounts available to the researcher, Drake's recorders claimed the navigator was under secret orders of Queen Elizabeth I. But many historians throughout the centuries did not believe this statement and have gone to great lengths to prove their adverse theory. One twentieth century scholar who believed that Francis Drake was under orders of the crown was Zelia Nuttall, author of *More Light On Drake*, a Hakluyt Society publication released in 1913. One of the enigmas of Drake's circumnavigation chronicles is the conflicting latitude heights in the north Pacific supposedly reached by Drake and his famous vessel, the *Golden Hinde*. Some records stated 43 degrees was the highest parallel reached. Others stated 45 degrees, and still others asserted the most northern point was 48 degrees, which would be approximately the latitude entrance of the Strait of Juan de Fuca. Mrs. Nuttall believed the trek reached into the far north, possibly into the waters of the Arctic Ocean. This writing will show the conjectures of the historian to be correct on both counts.

On the Oregon coast of the United States, there has been, for more than a century, another mystery concerning the sea. In the latter part of the nineteenth century, approximately the year 1885, early pioneers homesteading a bit of meadowland found—almost hidden in the tall grass—a few huge boulders with strange incised marks chiseled in the surface by man. The boulders were within a few yards of the ocean beach.

Another mystery of the area concerned the remains of an ancient ship scattered, and half-buried in the blowing sands, a few miles south of the engraved stones. Strewn along the sand spit near the old ship's remains were several tons of beeswax in the form of large cakes, as well as candles of varying sizes. The old wreck was found to have much teakwood planking in the hull, thus it was quickly determined that the derelict had originated in Asia. After much examination and many opinions by experts and would-be experts, the wax, too, was found to have originated on the opposite side of the Pacific Ocean.

Historical records indicated Spanish cargo vessels from the Philippine Islands and other places in the East Indies often made a landfall on the west coast of North America approximately in the latitude of Neah-Kah-Nie Mountain's location. The lumbering old tradeships traversed the Pacific currents for three hundred years before that route was abandoned.

Who can blame the Neah-Kah-Nie settlers for believing a "Manila Galleon" had crashed ashore at the foot of the mountain? Local seamen asserted that old galleon skippers, in the early days of world-wide trade, navigated without a knowledge of precise longitude, thus going ashore while on an east-west track was not uncommon. The next assumption from those who pondered the origin of the wreck was to believe that the marked rocks were the directions to buried treasure, for everyone knew that Spanish ships always carried gold. Perhaps it was not an off-course merchantman at all; perhaps it was a pirate ship loaded with treasure! Opinions concerning the combination of ship, wax, and marked boulders ran wild, but few men laughed because the evidence on the beach could not be denied.

The author was one of the many hundreds, who, through the years, pondered the mystery of Neah-Kah-Nie's strange relics. After decades studying the mountain and the records of the assaults on its inexplicable enigmas, I believed I had determined the meaning of the glyphs on the stones, which had come to be known as the "Treasure Rocks." Considerable more time and work proved me to be almost completely wrong, but my theories led me on the path to the ultimate solution of Neah-Kah-Nie's puzzles, which in turn revealed the answers to the mystery surrounding the 1577 voyage of Francis Drake.

Drake was an even greater mariner than his record admits. At Neah-Kah-Nie, he left behind a key to history that ranks equal to that of Egypt's famed Rosetta Stone.

Sir Francis Drake in 1586

FRANCIS DRAKE IN THE NEW WORLD

CHAPTER 1

FRANCIS DRAKE, WHO can justly be assigned the title "greatest mariner of all time and all nations," has a birth year veiled in the swirling obscure mists of uncertainty due to those early English times when records for commoners were not important. In fact, even the census of the gentry was subject to numerous hazards due to political turmoil and religious strife that tore all of Europe asunder during the Reformation era.

Perhaps an accurate record of Francis Drake's birth year can be determined from a portrait of Drake that hangs in Buckland Abbey at Plymouth. Drake purchased the estate in 1580, soon after his return from the circumnavigation. This painting can probably be deemed an official record because it was created in the seafarer's later years when he had periods of leisure long enough to sit for a portrait. The full-length painting's original inscription says "*aetatis suae 53*," along with the year it was finished. Thus we can determine that Drake was fifty-three years old at the time of the portrait, which means he was born in 1541.

Another painting of Drake, known as the "Miniature of Hilliard," also provides a birth record. The inscription on the small painting states it was completed in 1581 and that Drake was forty-two years old at that time. However, Hilliard somehow determined the captain was to have been born in either 1538 or 1539. It is conceded by most biographers that artist Hilliard was making a "best guess" at Drake's age. The miniature painted in 1581 was done immediate to the time of the mariner's return from his world-circling voyage, a time when his admirers were virtually unlimited in England.

Before his round-the-world voyage, Drake was already known as a harasser of the hated Spanish, and when he returned from a three-year jaunt around the globe, no words of praise were too high. Francis Drake appealed to the romantic imagination of all England. In this setting, Hilliard painted the miniature.

Because of the probable incorrectness of dates concerning the painting, it is entirely feasible that the artist sketched and painted the hero from somewhat afar on a catch-as-catch-can basis. The tiny portrait was done on the back of a piece of playing card, which appears to be the Ace of Hearts. One wonders if perhaps both Drake and Hilliard may have spent time at the same tavern or inn, or perhaps the artist made it a point to be at a place Drake frequented. Erroneous dates or not, the miniature is a historical treasure, a representation of all England's admiration for the renowned seaman.

Evidence other than the Buckland Abbey portrait exists indicating that Drake was born in 1541, so that date is probably correct.

The birth of the redheaded future sailor took place on Crowndale Farm near Tavistock, England. The father of the red-haired, blue-eyed infant was Edmund Drake, a part-time sailor, farmer, and preacher. Unfortunately, the name of Francis' mother is unknown. There is a cloudy record of the father's influence on his son, and so it must be to his mother that credit be given for many of Drake's manners, actions and ideals. It is generally a first-born son to whom a woman patiently teaches all she can to carefully mould him into her long-held image of what a great man should be. When looking at the manners, gestures, and obvious feelings of compassion in Francis Drake, it is undoubtedly the spirit of his mother that emerges. A father generally serves to influence his son's future occupations, work, and physical actions. Thus, for Francis Drake, we must conclude that it was his father's influence that led him down the trackless paths of the sea and committed him to the many courageous deeds in his future. Perhaps it was his mother who directed his hand in dealing with his associates and presented him with a desire to elevate his position in life. Both parents influenced his deep religious beliefs.

Crowndale Farm was under lease to Francis Drake's grandfather, John Drake. Edmund and his family occupied a laborer's cottage on the grounds. Edmund Drake came to the farm when he married Francis' mother. Being a sailor, and most probably without funds, Edmund may have found it necessary to rely on his father, John, for the first home of his new bride.

In later years, Francis Drake told the historian Camden that he was of "mean" parentage. Many writers and others have argued that this terminology meant he was born of middle class people. Others believe his parents were of a very low grade. Actually, a middle ground between the two definitions is probably correct. When one is a youngster in a seafaring town, as Francis Drake was, and your parents are part of the water life, one is forever conscious of the "others" who can afford to dress in fine clothes and live distant from the waterfront. The difference in living standards was something Francis Drake never forgot.

At most seaports, large and small, the land usually rises for some distance away from the water's edge. Merchants may have their business establishments on the main street close to the docks and sea, but they endeavored to live their private lives away from the rowdy element. Therefore, wealthier residents built their homes a distance from the water. For them, it was one thing to be part of the waterfront when making a living, but they preferred to enjoy their leisure hours "on the hill" where they could look down on the scene below and enjoy a beverage from a thin-walled glass and converse in a quiet atmosphere with a few select friends. It is for the sailor or dockworker to spend his evenings surrounded by the din and uproar of a noisy tavern, and to have a large, thick-walled mug of beer in the company of strangers just in on a vessel from another port.

For children of the waterfront, the people on the hill were disliked or even hated, no matter what changes life brought. Even as the youth grew to adulthood, the distinctions of class could rarely be forgotten. On rare occasions where invitations to a party at a nice home were offered, they would often hear references to "that awful waterfront," or "it smells down there," or, "I'm afraid of that place."

Sometimes the invitations stemmed from genuine friendliness—perhaps an association started between a merchant's child and a waterfront youngster, but the relationship seldom lasted. The child of the sea soon found his clothes to be too shabby and ill fitting in comparison to those of his newfound friend. Or, he would find himself continually embarrassed by his ignorance in handling the nice possessions of the "better" family. Often he would be too afraid to eat for fear his clumsiness with fragile tableware would bring him a warning from the matron of the house. He may even have found a girl he desired carefully guided away by her parents whenever she came to close to him. No one had to tell the child of the waterfront that his place in life was different from the elite living up the hill. Memories such as these are never forgotten. Quite possibly the old mariner who Francis Drake became was harking back to his discomfort about society when he said he was born of "mean parentage."

It may have been the efforts of Drake's mother that later developed the man's love for fine clothes, tableware and impeccable manners. It is not hard to imagine a good woman of modest means telling her son, "We may be poor, but that is no excuse for being dirty." Or, "Good manners are not only for those with fine possessions." Drake's parents may have been of low class, but the character foundation inherited from them was solid teaching that served him well throughout his life.

The farm of Crowndale was home to the Edmund Drake family until 1549. Edmund, Francis' father, was a devout protestant who preached his beliefs to all who would listen, whenever he found the opportunity. Being a sailor and a preacher is generally thought to be an odd combination, however many seamen, in spite of a rough life, are quite religious.

Confrontation, some of it violent, frequently occurred between the Catholics and Protestants in the Tavistock area. Edmund Drake's rough-and-ready seafaring background may have furnished him with an ability to be heard in any situation when carrying forth his message, thus his feelings and beliefs were well known in the community. Eventually, Edmund built up such a solid wall of Catholic animosity against his religious discourses that he was forced to leave the rural settlement and take his family to Plymouth in 1549. It was in this port where young Francis obtained his first taste of marine living.

The migration of the Drake family to Plymouth proved to be a trek into another hotbed of religious confrontations. Beyond question, the sailor-preacher Edmund contributed to the chaotic occasions. It was at this time that parliament decreed the English prayer book be put into use. Catholics were astounded that this insult should be added to a former proclamation that it was entirely lawful to give no credence to numerous Catholic beliefs and practices. The decree caused loud Catholic protest.

Edmund Drake and his family, as might be expected, bore a large share of the brunt of the Catholic feelings. The sailor, his wife, and their brood were unceremoniously run out of town and they took refuge on St. Nicholas Island in the harbor of Plymouth. The impeached mariner who had "got religion" made no effort to curtail his preachings and continued to loudly proclaim the Protestant doctrine to all who would listen, or could not refrain from hearing.

Francis Drake was eight years old by then, an age when events sometimes become deeply impressed upon a young person's mind. His hatred of the "papists" in his mature years is well known. Being chased from one home to another during his childhood could only have been deeply imbedded in his thoughts, thence placed in a memory never to be forgotten. Perhaps his father Edmund, in his zeal to promote his beliefs, brought much of his troubles upon himself, but Francis Drake's record makes it evident that he admired his father and that his sire's religious beliefs became his own. A young man adoring his father, while suffering much want because of eviction from his home and away from friends could not help but be remembered always. The fragile thread of record concerning Francis Drake's early life becomes even more fragmented for the following ten years.

Edmund and his wife, with their several offspring (how many exactly is not known, but eventually they had twelve children), retreated to the island of St. Nicholas with other tormented and troubled Protestants. Sir Thomas Cotton, with a clutch of crown small vessels, came to the aid of the destitute religious group who were by then very much in danger of death. William Hawkins, the great seafarer who Francis was associated with in his mature years, was a distant relative of the Drake family. He, too, came to their rescue and succor, taking the poverty-stricken castaways to the Medway.

The homeport for England's navy during that period was Gillingham Reach. The senior Drake was given the position of "bible reader" to the ship's companies. Being a preacher for the Tudor navy was only one small step above a starvation existence, especially for the good-sized family of Drakes. Not even a house on shore could be afforded by Edmund. Instead, a partially dismantled navy hulk was destined to be their home. In all probability, the hull had been scavenged of all its useable fittings, including yards and topmasts, as was the usual practice. Logically, the old and rotting hull was in shallow water at the edge of the beach, tied to an old piling or dolphin, in an area that ran dry on the ebb tide, then flooded to a depth of a foot or two at high water. A string of tied-together small logs and salvaged planking would form a walkway from the derelict vessel to dry land. Or, perhaps the hulk may have been tied to an abandoned quay where the water had shoaled to a degree that the dock was no longer useable for naval purposes. The old hull probably floated on extreme high tides, but most of the time remained stranded with the seawater trickling back and forth through many open seams whose caulking had rotted away many years ago. Undoubtedly, the cast-off ship and its hard-pressed group were on the far edge of the main naval activity.

The picture thus painted, to a landsman, may appear to be one of an abode of extreme squalidness and discomfort. The reverse of this could have been true. Most of the old naval vessels were extremely well constructed with thick, durable hardwoods. Most probably, the upper deck area where the Drakes lived was in sound condition. It was the underwater hull planking that deteriorated first on the sixteenth century men-of-war. In those early days, there were no good deterrents available for use against marine borers, which delighted in eating the bottoms out of wooden ships. Many vessels would have their undersides virtually made into giant sieves by those water-borne wood eaters, while the upper works of the ship remained as sound as the day the ship was constructed.

Edmund Drake was a sailor and a good family man. It is reasonable to believe the Drake family lived in quarters that were much more comfortable than many shore-side abodes because of the father's knowledge of how to keep the decks well caulked and waterproof. Being a naval preacher, he would have access to much stores discarded by the navy, which would have furnished ample useable material for repairs on his ship-home. Undoubtedly, Francis' mother must have longed for an abode on dry land, but the boys in the family presumably were quite happy on the decks of the old warship.

Francis Drake's boyhood may have included ragged clothes and his food fare might have been extremely plain and repetitious, but probably very few days on that naval waterfront were not filled with interest or excitement for the boy. His first acquisition of worldly goods would have been an old skiff or raft on which to paddle around the inlet. Once he had the means of transportation, he would quickly discover which vessels were good for a handout from the galley. Just as rapidly learned would be who and where to stay away from—people that might exploit a young man's labor by force, or those who would want service without remuneration.

His fishing opportunities and boating skills would have furnished many family meals. Numerous chances for jettisoned bits of damaged or leftover cargo, or marine stores, are afforded a waterfront boy. This, too, would have enhanced the family's living.

Being a preacher's son, whose teachings were considerably different than those of the average boy, must have produced many tests for a youth who daily faced opportunities to acquire small bits of merchandise left unwatched on the docks. There would also have been a compensating factor in which it would soon be recognized that the lad could be trusted, and thus favors would have been directed his way by ship captains and merchants.

At some point in his very young life, Francis was apprenticed to the captain of a coastal trading bark, said vessel plying the waters from the east coast of England to the ports of Holland. It is not known what his exact age was at this time, but a reasonable guess puts him at twelve years. Today, in the twentieth century, to go to sea at that age is akin to shipping a babe aboard a vessel. In Drake's time though, and indeed through the nineteenth century, a lad of twelve years was expected to work. Young Francis would have been ready at that age to take on the duties of an apprentice seaman. His life thus far had furnished him a background of seafaring knowledge. Already, he would have known the names of the many lines used to control the way of a sailing vessel, how to read a compass, how to seize or whip the ends of lines to prevent their fraying, and how to make various rope splices. His hands would have already known the feeling of extreme soreness from the monotonous task of "rolling oakum," the process of producing long, soft, rope-like strands of caulking material from discarded rope ends and rigging lines long past their point of safety, for this was a chore old salts could pawn off onto young would-be sailors. It was a price the young man willingly paid for the privilege of being allowed to listen to the old hands' dock-talk and their embellished tales of harrowing experiences at sea.

Although actual experience at the wheel of a hull at sea would have been minimal when Drake was apprenticed, he would probably have already made several short coast trips on which he had been allowed to steer in nice weather. The "trick at the wheel" is a thrilling experience for a young sailor and a monotonous way to acquire tired legs for the experienced hand. Past dockside training would now be of value to the new apprentice. Listening to the sailors gam around the docks provided useful knowledge on how to handle many situations concerning a ship at sea. Although not having the actual experience, reflex action resulting from listening to the sailors talk would have served him favorably when faced later with his own situations on the water.

Contrary to the thinking of many of Drake's biographers, Francis would have been well prepared for his new venture in life when he sailed out of the Medway as an apprentice seaman. Undoubtedly, the life was hard when compared with that of a shore-side boy. Most likely, the first storm he rode out in the coaster would have scared him, but that was not something he'd ever admit to anyone. The peril of huge, cold, green seas crashing aboard on one side of the small bark, thence to go foaming across the deck and roaring over the opposite rail, might have made young Francis wonder if his life might already be coming to an end. It would be then, with hands so cold and stiff that they ached like two large ulcerated teeth, with so little strength left that he could barely hold onto a line to keep himself from being washed over the side, that he prayed to be back home, aboard the old hull at the anchorage.

When one's clothes have not been dry for days and the bunk is a damp, cold, clammy mass; when one has been on his feet day and night without one single moment where he did not have to brace himself; and without letup having to hold onto a rail or line to prevent a pitch or roll of the vessel smashing him against a bulkhead, mast, or other unyielding part of the hull, it is then that any warm fire on any shore seems like heaven to a fool who sought the "romance of the sea."

Apprentice Drake would have experienced these feelings soon after he shipped out on the coaster. Survival is a first lesson for sailors. Prayers taught to him by a religious father would have come forth during his the first storm. If the blow was bad enough, even the roughest, toughest members of a crew would request the aid of someone greater than they to smooth down the icy, wild, black water.

The young mariner would also have soon learned that freezing, death-dealing storms are quickly lost from mind when the warm sun appears and quiet seas prevail. Dry clothes that have had the stiffening salt washed out of them, and a few hours sleep in a dried bunk that heaves slowly up and down with just the right amount of roll to make one sleep peacefully without having to brace knees against the sideboard, effectively eliminates all former thoughts of wanting to be ashore. When a steady breeze from the stern continued through clear days and bright, moonlight nights, perhaps it was then that Francis Drake firmly committed himself into the mold which later bestowed upon him the title of "World's Greatest Seaman."

When Francis was around seventeen, the fortunes of the Drake family changed for the better. Edmund Drake became Vicar of Upchurch and took his family ashore to live. It is doubtful that Francis ever stayed any length of time at the new home, but most certainly he must have periodically visited a few days when the bark was in port close by.

Shortly after his father was made Vicar, Francis Drake became master of his own ship. The captain to whom he had been apprenticed years before was a bachelor and during the years had become deeply attached to his young seaman. When the captain died, the bark was willed to Francis.

This gift is a first testimony to the dependability and seamanship of Drake. A man's ship is his most prized possession. Many seamen assert that is why a vessel is always referred to as being female, because like any woman worth having, she must continually be cared for and watched over. Decidedly, this would have been the case of the old master, for whom, being single, the small vessel must have virtually been his life. To will it to his young hand was tantamount to handing over his most precious belonging. It indicated that he trusted Francis and had complete faith his apprentice would continue to care for it.

Not only would Francis have understood the honor of such a trust, but perhaps more importantly, he would have received the recognition of the entire seafaring fraternity on the coastlines of the English Channel. News travels fast on the water and the old master's faith in the young sailor did not go unnoticed. Many times in his later years, this "first faith" in Drake was upheld and repeatedly asserted by acts of faithfulness by his crews.

Perhaps now is the proper place to size up Francis Drake, seaman. No longer an apprentice, yet not even twenty years old and in command of his own trading vessel, Drake certainly could have been called a seasoned sailor. There is a wide gulf and a vast difference, however, between seasoned sailor and seasoned captain. Undoubtedly, the young Englishman had conned the bark in and out of various ports, stood at the helm in storm-wracked seas, and relied on his own judgment in many marine situations. There is a difference, however, between making crucial decisions at sea with an old veteran sea captain at your shoulder, and making them when you are all alone. Especially when your efforts may mean life or death for your vessel and crew, and when, with no more-experienced mind to correct you, your fortune could disappear within a few moments.

The first few trips across the English Channel were trying ones for Britain's future man of the hour. Always before, when a headland appeared out of the mists, Drake could recognize and state the name of the landmark with confidence, for the old captain was nearby to correct him if he should happen to be mistaken. The aged master had been Drake's safety valve. Once the captain was gone, when out of the cold spume and fogs momentarily appeared a promontory, there were no affirmative or negative remarks from one of greater experience to bolster Drake's confidence. But the new captain had learned well from the old skipper. A sharp devil-may-care attitude probably received an initial blunting as the ship's new master took in some sail, slowed the way of the hull, and headed the stem further out to sea—just in case his reckoning had been wrong. Francis Drake's sole responsibility for his craft most likely did not produce the feeling of utmost confidence. He had never been one hundred percent responsible before and he became cautious, arriving in port a day later than expected. Some of his arrogant confidence would have diminished, replaced by the initial training for his globe-circling voyage, as yet undreamed.

In 1561, or approximately that year, Drake's name started to become widely known throughout Europe. During the ensuing decades, Spain and England would be at each other's throats. Religious differences, and the aggressive attitudes regarding the conquering of new lands in a world newly opened to exploration, would bring the two countries together in clash after clash of political jousts and bloody armed conflicts. Spain would eventually be the first to fall. But this peninsula country was destined to gain control over a huge part of the globe before internal strife and weakness deteriorated its globe-encompassing Catholic domain. Spain's collapse shrank its boundaries, returning the country to almost the original lines drawn in the fifteen century when Columbus opened the door for its westerly expansion.

The triumphant British took up where Spain left off. England also became too large and cumbersome for controlled government; their seams were to eventually burst in a similar manner as those of the deposed Iberians.

Francis Drake matured into the festering thorn that led to the eventual downfall of Spain. His father's religious influence made him a zealous Protestant sea captain who never missed a chance to sink a Spanish ship, sack a Spanish city, or in battle give a helping hand to an Iberian who might be persuaded to leave this world. His dedication was reciprocated in full by Spain's diplomats, soldiers, and any other Spaniard who had heard his name. Few hadn't. Drake's religious stand was blasted by every Catholic representative who could invent a new title for him without taking the Lord's name in vain. One Jesuit padre called him "Devil Drake." It was the worst name the pious man could bring himself to call the Englishman.

CHAPTER 2

Francis Drake became the owner of the bark at a crucial time in the history of Europe. The lowlands, now known as Holland, had been under the influence of the Holy Roman Empire for many centuries. By marriage and political maneuverings, Spanish influence injected itself in the fifteenth century when Charles V of the Spanish branch of the house of Hapsburg became the ruling power.

In 1555, Philip II, son of Charles, took over the reins. His dislike for the people in the North European lands of his kingdom resulted in oppressive government of the Dutch. Then Holland came under complete control of the infamous Spanish Inquisition. Citizens suspected of heresy against the Catholic Church, or of plotting against the crown, were imprisoned and tortured; many times without benefit of any hearing or trial.

When Francis was twenty years old, it had been twenty-four years since Martin Luther nailed his famous thesis to the door of the Castle Church of Wittenberg, thus creating the beginning of the Reformation. In 1533, John Calvin picked up the torch of reform to spread his beliefs and protest for religious change. The reform movement was fast spreading across Europe by 1561.

Flemish refugees by the hundreds fled England where the young Queen Elizabeth I welcomed them with sheltering arms. During this period, a youthful, religious Protestant captain, full of daring, with a will to back up his beliefs, assuredly must have loaded his small vessel to capacity numerous times to bring refugees to England and a new life. In them, he saw his own plight from just a few years past.

It was a relatively good life, plying back and forth across the channel with assorted cargos. Drake's sturdy bark was not only a means of earning a living, it also furnished a bed and place to live when tied to the dock. The life was a carefree one for a young sailor. His trips were not exceedingly long enough to cause the sea to become monotonous and boring. Length of time away from port was just enough for the harbor entrance to promise new interest and excitement when he came ashore again.

Life on a small boat is quite different from that of any other environment, especially when the sea is lumpy and rough. After a few days of continual bracing the body for balance, both when awake and when asleep, a sailor quite often changes from a happy near-boisterous man to a quiet, withdrawn individual. Long-distance sailors often silently wish to be back ashore, mentally cussing the cold, green, roughed-up surface that ceaselessly bangs and thumps the hull in a continuous effort to either dump the noonday meal on the galley floor, loosen the lashings on a boom so it can thrash to pieces some of the upper works, or produce an exaggerated plunging roll to wake one's sleep. For some men, a prolonged trip of stormy seas and aggravating happenings changes them from an easy-going person into a savage animal. It is best to stay away from such a person, but that becomes a chore of great difficulty when living on a small vessel. In turn, this same man is usually a fine seaman who will always do his work with expertise, and can be totally relied upon in any emergency circumstance. When the trip is over and this man steps ashore, he once again becomes a congenial companion. Ask him why he goes to sea when it affects him in such a manner and he will be unable to furnish an answer. He has asked himself the same question many times without reaching a reasonable conclusion.

No matter that the man on the water becomes anxious to step ashore after a voyage. The solid ground he looked forward to so anxiously soon becomes a boring place of noisy humanity where the shore-side men never cease to flap their mouths and utter continuous babble with very little meaning. The silence of the sea begins to beckon and the man begins to drop hints at various waterfront establishments that he is available as a hand if someone will beg him long enough. Usually, the first of a crew to do this is the sailor who outwardly hates the sea so bad and becomes miserable while on a trip.

During his late teens and early twenties, Francis Drake, with his handy coasting bark, was tempered like a fine piece of sword steel. He was built for a life of reliability and service to England on the seas of the globe. The years of short channel crossings disallowed any chance for his disgust or boredom of the water. His life was in continual change, from interest and excitement on land, to the exhilarating freedom when once again on the deck. This important period of his training, carried forth in progressive steps, nurtured his dreams and love of water he'd been exposed to as a boy on the waterfronts of Plymouth and Medley.

In 1564, Drake received the next stage of his sea training. He was by then twenty-three years old. Behind him were eleven years of water experience, five of them as master of his own vessel. At this time, the Catholic/Protestant feud, now essentially between England and Spain, had projected itself to a savage inhuman intensity wherein all men's lives were in jeopardy whenever representatives of the two countries met.

The Hawkins family, Drake's distant seafaring relations, were in the maritime trading business on an ocean-crossing scale. Although the sea would never become boring to Francis, he had crossed and re-crossed the English Channel so many times it seemed like just a mere puddle. Its headlands and currents were so familiar, there was no longer a challenge in the rough shores and stormy surface. The long tracks of the Hawkins' ships beckoned to him. Hawkins' vessels were heading to the African west coast and the far off West Indies, places of adventure that Francis Drake had heard of many times, but never had the chance to see for himself.

Substantial literary confusion enters the account of

Drake's life at this point. Historians disagree as to whether Drake sold his bark or leased it out. One record has it that King Philip of Spain closed all ports of Holland to English trade, thus forcing all British captains out of cross-channel trading to the lowlands. One chronicle states that this move of the Iberian monarch was cause for Drake to sell his vessel.

It is doubtful the little trading bark was disposed of at this time. If business had stopped or come to a near standstill for channel traders, it is considerably more feasible that the bark was laid up for a period of time while Drake shipped out on one of the Hawkins' vessels. It is rare for a one-vessel ship owner to sell his craft unless he has in mind the purchase of a larger or better one.

Francis Drake signed aboard as purser on a vessel bound for the Biscayan coast of Spain. His bark was in all probability put in the charge of his deckhand or some reliable shore-side resident while it was laid up at a mooring during the Spanish closure of the Dutch ports. There is also the possibility of arrangements having been made wherein the bark could be put into service if the opportunity presented itself while the owner was away. It is doubtful the little ship was sold at that time.

There is small difference in circumstances for a sailor, be it in the sixteenth century or the twentieth. When the pockets become empty and food and drink cannot be purchased, then one must find a berth where bed and grub are furnished. Drake's business had come to a halt, at least temporarily. His pockets were bare, but he had relatives in the business and his blood ties could be instrumental in securing a berth. Presumably, the chance to visit strange seas and new lands influenced his choice of shipping out.

The fact that he shipped out as a purser, a position of trust on a trading vessel, attests once again to the reliability of the man's character. Being a relative of William Hawkins could have obtained a seaman's berth, but there had to be additional reason to be designated as purser.

Little is know about Drake's first voyage on Hawkins ship. Ironically, he had barely signed the ship's articles when the Spanish embargo was lifted. Other than the opportunity to learn new coastlines and see strange places, there may have been other reasons for Drake to make this passage. He could have been a spy sent to look and listen for anything and everything.

If, at the time of his signing on the Hawkins craft, English/Spanish relations were at such an extremely low point as to have the Flemish ports closed to the British, then it must have been very special circumstances that allowed the vessel Drake was on to enter a port of Spain. Rigid controls were undoubtedly imposed upon the English sailors when cargo was being unloaded and new freight taken aboard.

If not restricted to their vessel by law, most of the crew may have voluntarily stayed aboard because of risk to life and limb ashore. Spanish military personnel, some members of the Inquisition, and other patriotic citizens would have found extreme pleasure in eliminating any English sailor they could catch ashore.

Conversely, the seas of Europe contained a large number of English rovers who liked nothing better than to capture a Spanish vessel and put her papist crew to the sword. No "walking the plank" here. That was a game with too much uncertainty. One of the hated Spanish dogs might somehow survive the plunge, which could not be tolerated. Instead, they would tie the spike-bearded sailor to the middle of a line, then saw him back and forth across the keel, under the hull, from one side of the vessel to the other until the lifeless, barnacle-shredded body could no longer hold together. Or, if there was not enough time for this horseplay, they simply ran the Spaniards through several times with their swords and kicked the men overboard!

Spanish ships, capturing an English hull, had seamen aboard equally adept at ridding the seas of unwanted English heretics. The Spaniards amused themselves by decapitating the Englishmen and then climaxing the job by drawing and quartering the carcasses in the manner of a pork or beef. The resulting pieces made great attractions for hungry gulls and other sea birds. No greater enjoyment could be imagined than to have a wandering shark stop and show his liking for a chopped Englishman.

Such was the type of hatred prevailing on the seas

between the Spanish and English, thus the vessel carrying Drake as purser must have been at dock in an extremely tense atmosphere. Francis Drake, with his preacher-father and Protestant background, was perhaps the most religiously biased of all men on board. This facet of character added fuel to the fires of hatred for the Spanish that the average English Protestant carried in his breast.

The year 1565 marked another turning point in the career of the soon to be predominant "thorn in the side" of Spain. Cousin John Hawkins was making a name for himself in another trading venture that was far more lucrative than packing ordinary trade goods back and forth along the European coasts in a monotonous cape-to-cape track, there and back along the same routes. The African slave trade was by far a more exciting venture and the profits were commensurate. Slave trading in the sixteenth century was considered an honorable occupation by all European countries. The excitement and adventure of such a voyage appealed to the daredevil Drake, and the high profits were certainly to his liking.

When Pope Alexander so generously, and with such great wisdom, divided the world in half by simply stating so, and by giving equal portions to Spain and to Portugal, he may have unknowingly instigated the primary energizer to England's expansive colonial system. English territory became so large that it earned the slogan "upon which the sun never sets." Alexander, in one grandiose move of stultification, had not only hypothetically halved the earth, but also contributed to the splitting of Europe into two armed camps. The soon-powerful new group of religious zealots pitted themselves against the Catholic domination of Europe. Protestants like Drake used every chance and means to deliver a crippling blow against the papists.

Although written records indicate atrocities and hatreds perpetrated by the Spanish and English during this period of history, other people suffered far worse at the hands of the Catholics and Protestants.

To wage a conflict in Europe during the 1500s, regardless of whether it was an armed meeting of forces or simply war conducted by trade monopolies, the confrontations required large amounts of capital. And this need was not relegated solely to fighting nations. The hidden conflicts between the two religious factions also had need of funds. Gold and silver were then the controlling mediums of exchange, just as they are today.

When Columbus stumbled onto a new land with his three little bulbous-nosed vessels, a Pandora's box was opened and remains open to this day. Almost immediately after Columbus, a Portuguese who became an agent of Spain funded by Queen Isabella, reported his discovery, other Spanish sea captains journeyed to the newly found lands and brought large amounts of precious metals back to the Iberian peninsula.

Christopher Columbus expected to sail straight to China and the East Indies when he left the eastern side of the Atlantic in 1492. Indeed, according to records, he presumed that the islands of the East Indies were his landfall when he sighted the emerald keys of the Gulf of Mexico. With this false conception in mind, it was natural for Columbus to call the natives of his first anchorage "Indians," a name that has clung to them ever since.

Historical records indicate that most often it was white men who made slaves of those with darker skins. Some of the most bigoted reasoning claims that dark skin makes people inferior, which is, of course, not true. It has been the more aggressive and ambitious peoples, with their cloaked savageness, who made slaves of the gentler groups in the world. The coincidence of making slaves of many African tribes and numerous groups of North and South American Indians, all of whom were of a tolerant nature, has led to much of the warped thinking.

Survival needs in Europe during past centuries bred a fierce competitive drive into the people living in that part of the globe. Every day they vied with the harshness of nature in an effort to feed and clothe themselves. In most of Europe, cold winters and short summers are not conducive to agricultural abundance. The climate requires considerable effort to obtain clothing and shelter sufficient to combat the bleak winter landscape. Although the seas along the coastline were teaming with an abundance of fish, the waters were rough and choppy and fishing was difficult for the English, French, Dutch, and others who dared to venture forth for their fare.

When the daring seamen of Spain and Portugal embarked upon their quest for new worlds, it was into the tropical lands they first ventured, which is where they found animal and vegetable abundance. The tropic people had little need to compete with each other for survival; hence most of them were mild-tempered, openhearted tribes who graciously welcomed the Europeans to their shores.

The gold and silver originally found by the Spanish in the gulf regions of the new "Indies" was, for the most part, in the form of manmade objects such as body ornaments, small idols, dishes, and tools. These artifacts were quickly wrested from the natives by the "conquistadors." The amount of loot taken from the Aztec and Inca nations was enormous. In the course of this robbing of Indian nations, Spain became a wealthy and powerful nation and her need for gold and silver increased steadily as she exerted more and more economic pressure and power upon the rest of Europe.

Faced with a decline in her treasury holdings and large expenditures that could no longer be funded by the confiscation of Inca and Aztec belongings, and not wishing to assume a lesser position of power, the high-riding Spanish reasoned that their only recourse to maintaining their wealth and power was to mine the metals of the new world. Many good outcroppings of silver and placer gold had been discovered by the far-roving conquistadors.

Mining the lands of North and South America required large amounts of hand labor. Hard work has never been a prime asset of politicians or soldiers and the Spaniards had a dim view of physical exertion. The combination of gentle Indian tribes and tough adventurous conquistadors soon resulted in mining camps containing thousands of Indian slaves.

The farmlands of Spanish settlers were confiscated in order to feed those working the ore lodes in the earth. The miners were fed only enough to keep them alive, but still this policy required vast amounts of food. Thousands of Indian workers died each year from disease, insufficient food, and by overwork. Many Indians at the mines were killed in cold blood by their Spanish overlords when they refused to work. Monotonous, steady work was an alien part of the American Indian's makeup. Rebellion at the "reales," or mines, increased steadily. This, along with the death of so many slaves, began to produce a steady decline in mineral production.

It was discovered that the best miner was the Negro. He was a patient, plodding, hardworking underground laborer who complained little. The Spaniards were quick to take advantage of this labor force and soon depopulated the Caribbean islands of its healthy Negroes by transporting them to the mainland areas where they were sent to mines or put to work on farms and cattle ranches.

When men are engaged in making profits, everything else must take a place of lesser importance. Even the hatred of Catholics against Protestants was set aside long enough for products and monies to change hands between Englishmen and Spaniards.

Thus, the circle was complete. Spanish control in Europe forced the British to become more aggressive and John Hawkins became a dealer in African slaves, selling them to Spaniards in the new world who were buying those slaves against their King's orders. The Iberian monarch made only feeble protest because these black men were going to the mines where they would dig more gold and silver for Spain.

Slave trading was a lucrative business. The lure of huge profits made by his relative John Hawkins was undoubtedly a factor in changing the course for Drake. As previously stated, slavery in the sixteenth century was considered an honorable profession by most, so the venturesome Francis Drake, always eager to make a profit, entered the trade. It turned out this decision had a great bearing on the most important emancipation of slavery in all time.

It would be Drake's claim to western North America on which England would rely, and in turn would contribute to Spain's retirement from the area. While Drake helped place many men into slavery on one early voyage, a future journey contributed to the freeing of hundreds of thousands of indentured men.

The Spanish crown endeavored to control the African slave trade for Spaniards only. Spaniards in the new world were forbidden to buy slaves from anyone other than a fellow Spaniard licensed by King Philip. Caribbean Spanish officials, always willing to make a sideline profit, were somewhat prone to look the other way if an English ship unloaded human cargo in one of the southern ports. John Hawkins had a system worked out with a few crown representatives whereby when he arrived at a West Indies island to sell a cargo, he would land a small contingent of armed men for a show of force and then stage a mock attempt at raiding the local settlement. The corrupt Spanish official who governed the town would sally forth with his troops to fire a volley at the English, making sure that the range was too far for the guns to do any damage. Hawkins would then in turn have his men fire a similar devastating barrage at the distant Iberians. When both sides had contributed their part of the enacted battle, and the populace had retreated into the jungle, the Spanish military force would find it necessary to withdraw to the woods for the protection of the townspeople.

In the evening, under cover of darkness, John Hawkins and the Spanish gentlemen would carry out their business transactions. It was a lucrative arrangement for all concerned except for King Philip of Spain who, of course, was deprived of his share of license monies.

The slaving trade antics between his subjects and the English made Philip furious, but there was little he could do. After all, if questioned, his officials could prove the local garrison had done its best trying to resist the landing of the English while affording the protection of his people. The very fact that the town had not been devastated was certainly proof in itself that the governor and his troops did effectively give enough show of force to keep the invaders from raiding the city. Perhaps it could even be said that the official and his men had won the battle!

CHAPTER 3

FRANCIS DRAKE SAILED on his first slavery trade voyage in 1566. John Hawkins had fitted out four ships to sail on that South Atlantic venture and the preparation for the voyage required considerable time, all of which had not gone unnoticed by ever-inquisitive Spanish representatives stationed in England. King Philip, receiving notice of the preparations, visualized the audacious British captain again stealing away with a large amount of unpaid license fees due to the crown. So Spain's ambassador to England complained to the British court. Hawkins was summoned to appear before the Board of Admiralty, which positively forbade him to engage in a slaving venture. Perhaps the reproof of the board was only for political window dressing, or maybe Hawkins had little appreciation for their jurisdiction over waters so far from home, but in spite of the Admiralty Board's orders and possible subsequent political reverberations, the John Hawkins flotilla sailed on its trading venture with Francis Drake on one of the decks.

Cousin John Hawkins abided in part by the decree of the Admiralty Board. He did not sail with his group of vessels. Instead, the ships were placed under the command of Captain John Lovell. Little is known of this voyage except that it was a financial failure.

While cruising the shores of African Guinea to obtain a cargo of slaves, Lovell and the Portuguese entered into several sea battles. The Portuguese claimed ownership of those shores, consequently rightly viewing that the English captain as a marauder and pirate. After battling his way from the African coast by way of Cape Verde and the Azores, Lovell's subsequent arrival in the Caribbean Sea gave him the position to extract a profit from the voyage. He made sales from the human cargo at the islands of Margarita, Burboroata, and Curacao. The last stop was at the town of Rio de la Hacha, where ninety slaves were hauled aboard.

Once more lady luck turned her fickle back on the fortuneless expedition. The mayor of the Spanish town, Miguel de Castellanos, confiscated the last of the African cargo in the name of the crown, paying not one coin for them. Undoubtedly, Castellanos, under normal conditions, was not above "business as usual" with the English smugglers, but apparently at that time he was out of favor with his superiors and seized upon this chance to place himself in a better light. Lovell was furious, but there was nothing to do but accept the loss and sail away.

It was not in character for John Lovell to accept a defeat such as this without strenuous resistance. He may have been a poor businessman and diplomat in his contacts during the voyage, but coward he was not. Before arriving in the Caribbean, he was able to beat off the Portuguese three times, clearly exhibiting his mettle.

The English captain must have recognized the existence of a delicate political situation in the unexpected seizure and had decided resistance would gain nothing in this case and possibly lose a great deal for future trading ventures. When his profitless fleet dropped anchor once more in English water, John Hawkins accepted the loss philosophically, saying only that it was because of "the lack of experience of my representatives."

There was one member of the just-returned expedition who found it impossible to brush aside the monetary loss so easily. Francis Drake had envisioned a handsome profit for himself when he shipped out on his relative's venture and he was beside himself with rage at the treachery of the hated Spanish. The two-handedness of the town's leader, Miguel de

Castellanos, helped convert the curly, red-haired young Englishman into what was to be the greatest Spanish adversary of all time. Every fiber in Drake's stocky young frame burned and thirsted for revenge. He vowed the Spanish would pay dearly for their trading treachery.

In 1567, Europe was a gigantic cauldron of boiling, churning, political intrigues and turmoil. Added to this dangerous concoction, which always contained untold thousands of treacherous ingredients, was the doubly intricate mixture of religious plots and wars. As with any well-cooked gumbo, it was virtually impossible to separate a political ingredient without the flavor and coloring of church elements clinging to it.

England, with her population widely split by the Catholic and Protestant religions, was perhaps the hottest spot in the maelstrom of deals, plots, double-crosses and all the other niceties that come along with the turmoil of endeavoring to construct a more powerful and better nation.

The pious King Philip of Spain was taking every opportunity to widen all cracks of difference that appeared in Queen Elizabeth's government of England. The Spanish monarch's spies and representatives were everywhere in the isles and were not without support of many Englishmen.

All of this cold warring was, of course, cloaked with an outward showing of charm and grace between English politicians and the official Spanish diplomats and representatives. Quite conceivably, while an Englishman was entertaining a watchful Spanish ambassador at tea, a fellow Britain down at the harbor would be taking advantage of the Spaniard's preoccupation by loading a ship with guns, shot, and powder to be used in the taking of a Spanish galleon loaded with gold and silver obtained in the new world.

Or, perhaps while a Protestant minister was entertained at a function, opposing factions were using Spanish gold to finance the burning of his unattended church. The vast riches of North America were well known by this time, with the fight for the new land affecting every European household. The English housewife had no way of knowing religious disputes with her neighbor were indirectly connected with a

Spanish dragoon being run through by a British sword on a far off Central American coastline. Nor would the Spanish matron have any way of realizing that her purchase of spices at the marketplace be associated with a gold-laden galleon traveling up from Mexico, or a musket ball entering the brain of an English seaman trying to scale the heaving side of his ship while under attack.

Thus was the situation of the Atlantic shores when once again John Hawkins prepared for a trading venture.

GOLDEN HINDE

CHAPTER 4

ENGLAND'S QUEEN ELIZABETH I was a monarch of remarkable ability. Her responsibilities were tremendous. She had inherited the reins of a nation burdened with an agricultural economy in a northern latitude more hostile than compatible to the growing of foodstuffs. Wool production gave forth a trade item of some value, but it required vast acreages for the raising of sheep and large numbers of animals to support just a few people. So hampering to the people was this part of the economy, that even in the sixteenth century, colonies were planned in North America because the "kingdom was overcrowded"!

In Tudor times, a lesser part of the economy was the production of coal and iron and their resulting products. This was a direct reverse of later times when manufacturing produced the world's strongest nation two centuries afterwards.

Spain had a throttle hold on the island nation of England, for she controlled not only the mainland of western Europe, but also the trade lanes of the Mediterranean Sea. True, some of the exotic products from the Far East could be obtained by Britain, but these items commanded prices affordable to only the very wealthy. By the time a Spanish-controlled trader finally sold a cargo to a British merchant, the price had sometimes increased twenty fold. This trade monopoly, combined with the immense mineral riches of the new lands of the Western Hemisphere, tended to increase Spain's power.

England, in contrast, was kept poor by her geographical situation. To openly contest Spain for a share of the world's riches would have been sheer madness and an unthinkable proposition for poverty-ridden England. An open contest required many ships, men, and arms, all of which in turn necessitated great sums of money. Elizabeth had none of these at her command.

Called "Good Queen Bess" by her admirers, and "a stingy old maid" by her detractors, the feisty, red-headed Elizabeth's chore to build a better nation was one of the most difficult any conscientious leader of any nation could face.

Spain was naturally jealous of her world position. Her king and other leaders had no intention of allowing any other nation to obtain even a small part of the land they controlled. She knew if any monarch should attempt to wrest away part of the Spanish domain, the wrath of King Philip's extreme power would be felt immediately.

Few events of importance to international affairs escaped the notice of Ambassador de Silva, Spain's leading emissary in England. His spies were everywhere, bringing to his attention any and all news of events that might possibly prove to be of gain to the Spanish crown.

Elizabeth and her supporting ministers had no choice. If England was to make progress in acquiring life's material comforts, she must obtain them by any means possible. Thus, the greatest "cold war" of all times began because of her people's needs; the same reason for all cold wars before and since. Elizabeth's unspoken policy was that the British would obtain the gold, silver, and trade items controlled by the Iberians by any means other than armed confrontation against ships or properties owned by the king of Spain.

Many Englishmen hotly disagreed with Elizabeth's mode of operation, wanting to charge directly at the Spanish and "blow them off the map." These men, of course, were those of lesser knowledge concerning the overall strengths of both the British and Spanish nations. Undoubtedly, most of them were brave enough to carry forth their ideals and would have been willing to die in the effort, but reprisal many times over would have been the only result of their foolish deeds. The best and only way to elevate the English way of life was political intrigue, assisted by daring and prudent seamen who understood the nation's necessity for advancing boldly only to the delicate apex where the most could be gained. They understood that armed conflict with the crown of Spain and its dominions and representatives must be averted.

For the queen, this was a hazardous situation. It was one thing to be responsible for ambassadors schooled in the delicate deceptions of court policies wherein the closest encounter with violence these people normally met would be a tilting of a nose construed as a public snubbing. Apologies to smooth the ruffled feelings of a foreign diplomat were commonplace and easy to come by.

However, to be responsible for a fiery, never-back-down sea captain who wouldn't give a damn for anyone's delicate nature, and who wouldn't hesitate to blow the sheerstreaks clean off a Spanish crown vessel, was a far different matter. It is no surprise that England's great seamen of these times had deep respect for their female leader. Sailors know only too well their frailties in the matters of shore-side diplomacy. No matter how loud they got in their disapproval of Elizabeth's policies, they knew to a man that any one of them could easily commit an act, during their encounters with the Spanish, that their queen would have to answer for. Perhaps because they knew she would back them, regardless of how foolish an act they might commit, the English sea captains transformed into better than average water-borne diplomats. To operate on a policy of "do anything and everything to take away from the Spanish, but don't make him mad enough for outright war" appears to have been the instructions from the English ministers to their ship captains. This was a delicate maneuver entrusted to a group of men whose life and environment were not conducive to such diplomacy.

It was a fiery, shoot-first-and-talk-later twenty-two year old Francis Drake who joined the Hawkins expedition of 1567. Unknown to the young mariner, the events to come would serve to temper his wild bravery and bold sailing aptitude into what earned him the name of "Devil" by the Spanish due to his well-disciplined courage, diplomacy, and superbly calculated seamanship.

For his new expedition, John Hawkins had obtained from the queen the loan of two great ships of the Royal Navy: the *Jesus of Lubeck*, seven hundred tons; and the *Minion*, three hundred and fifty tons. The *Jesus* was more than thirty years old, having literally been resurrected from "rotten row" to serve with Hawkins. Even so, the old ship carried twenty-two large pieces of armament, making a gun platform worthy of consideration should any adversary contest Hawkins' trading ventures. The smaller vessel, *Minion*, also added firepower in proportion.

While the great quantities of store were being loaded onto the two naval vessels and four other ships in the fleet, namely the *William and John*, at one hundred fifty tons, the *Swallow* at one hundred tons, the *Judith* at fifty tons, and the *Angel* at thirty-two tons, there was considerable harbor shuffling to be done to bring the hulls to the quays and take them back again to anchorages. This activity did not fail to arouse the interest of De Silva who immediately requested audience with Queen Elizabeth.

Hawkins' somewhat surreptitious slave trading in the West Indies in defiance of Spanish law was well known to the Iberian officials, so a loud and vigorous protest was made to the queen over the use of Royal Navy ships by the profit-seeking mariner. Elizabeth, of course, quickly denied to the Spanish ambassador that her vessels would be any part of a slave-trading voyage, especially one that would conflict with King Philip's royal order. She assured De Silva that the old naval ships were simply insurance against attacks from pirates who might wish to take advantage of a peaceful merchant venture.

Unquestionably, the red-haired British monarch would share in the profits of the venture; her investment was typical of the shrewd businesswoman. Hawkins had been leased two old maritime graveyard tubs long past their prime as commissioned naval vessels. To put them in useable shape for a trading voyage required extensive repairs and patchwork, all expenses, which had to be borne by Hawkins. Whatever share the queen would gain from the enterprise would be pure profit.

De Silva was in no way taken in by the assurances of the wily Elizabeth. She, too, was of well-known character and considered by the Spanish to be a dangerous adversary. A message of warning was hastily sent to King Philip, providing details of the marine preparations and of De Silva's audience at the castle.

Anchors were pulled and sails unfurled on October 2, 1567. Francis Drake was in command of the small fifty-ton *Judith*. The bark belonged to Drake, possibly having been purchased by selling his old bark, the *Zeeland*, from his channel trading days.

Slave buying on the Guinea coast of Africa was not profitable. The most favorable place for a slaving vessel to heave-to was normally at a river mouth where small boats could be taken inland, but this was not to prove true for the Hawkins venture. The blacks had become knowledgeable about slavers and their tactics of obtaining cargo, so when a sail was sighted, or the rattle of an anchor chain heard, the word was passed and the native people went inland, away from the waterway.

Only one hundred and fifty slaves had been captured or purchased when an opportunity to assist an African chief in his fight against another Guinea monarch netted Hawkins five hundred more units to his human cargo, and the voyage began to take on the prospect of high profit. Then, a Portuguese vessel, the *Grace of God*, was captured and this windfall gained the English adventurers a spanking new vessel of one hundred and fifty tons; a considerable addition to the small fleet. Undoubtedly, the leaky, pump-every-hour warship *Jesus* had earned its way.

Parts of the record for John Hawkins' third voyage are missing. There is mention of seven Portuguese caravels being driven ashore and captured at Rio Grande, but nothing to indicate how much, if any, booty was obtained from them.

Although the ships had more space available for additional slaves, it was decided that enough were aboard to declare their voyage a profitable venture. Yards were braced and bowstems pointed for the Caribbean. Fifty-five days later the fleet arrived in the clear blue waters of the West Indies.

A bit of leisurely trading was effected with various Spanish island communities, usually accomplished by the previously explained "Hawkins Method" whereby the local governor would fire cannons at the "invaders" and Hawkins would return the fire with both factions careful to ensure their targets were far out of range before fire was set to the powder. After the exchange of fire, Hawkins sailed out of sight. That evening, under cover of darkness, slaves and other goods were landed where Spanish merchants waited. The governor received a small tax on the transactions, and everyone was happy with their fair profit. Everyone but Spain's King Philip, of course.

By then marine grass and other sea growth had profusely coated the bottom of several of Hawkins' ships. Puerto Cabello was selected as a careening ground for scraping and oiling the hulls. The little vessels were more easily careened than the larger ones, and quickly freed of their travel-impeding growth.

Francis Drake had longed for a return bout with Castellanos, the slave stealer who had robbed him of his profit share from the previous voyage. When John Hawkins elected to send the already careened *Judith* and *Angel* ahead to the Rio de la Hacha for the opening of trade negotiations, one does not have to strain mental faculties to imagine his carrot-topped lieutenant having some influence on the decision. Perhaps Drake would have an opportunity to settle some scores. From this far distance in time, it is difficult to ascertain the reason for sending the *Judith* and *Angel* ahead, but perhaps Hawkins reasoned that the double-dealing Spaniard, Castellanos, needed a little tempering before actual trading began. His young nephew, Francis Drake, was just the person to arrange the proper atmosphere. The leader of the expedition could not have been more correct in his judgment.

With boldness that later became a trademark of his character, Drake sailed in close to Rio de la Hacha and anchored directly in front of the town. The usual greeting was given by the Spanish, who shot three times in the direction of the English ships, carefully ensuring their aim was wide of the mark. Nothing was harmed but the tranquility of the sea's glassy surface. The return fire from the *Judith* and *Angel* was somewhat different. Drake placed a roundshot that went completely through the governor's house. To add a final disdainful touch to his arrival, Drake also captured a small Iberian dispatch vessel arriving from Santo Domingo. This boat he apparently drove ashore by his mere presence, a situation he corrected by going in after the vessel and retrieving it from under the guns of the Spanish soldiers. Again he defiantly anchored in front of the town.

After a four-day wait, the sails of the *Jesus* and the rest of Hawkins' fleet topped the horizon. Hawkins could claim not being responsible for Drake's actions as he was not on the scene, and this he did immediately upon arrival. After all, he was on a peaceful trading voyage and confrontation with the Spanish was strictly against the queen's orders. The dispatch boat was released with apologies. Official narratives do not mention grog being issued to all hands as soon as the Spaniards were out of sight, but that is not too far-fetched a supposition.

Trading operations then proceeded smoothly, with most of the remaining Africans disposed of to Spanish merchants. Conceivably, other goods were traded as well. Francis Drake did not regain previous financial losses from Castellanos, but most certainly the holes in the governor's house must have provided some satisfaction for the intrepid young seaman.

With approximately fifty blacks and other small amounts of cargo left to sell, the squadron moved on to Cartagena and thence on a homeward route. It was August by then and the storm season of the gulf caught up with the English flotilla. The violent winds, accompanied by huge foaming seas, strained the old planking of the "tender" *Jesus* to the point where it began to leak like a sieve. The pumps were barely able to keep the vessel afloat even when working around the clock.

Hawkins' ships were then near the western end of Cuba and a port to put into for repairs was urgently needed. The extreme danger of their situation convinced Hawkins to put into the harbor of San Juan de Ulloa, the guardian fortress of Vera Cruz, Spain's principal city on the east coast of Mexico.

This port was the embarkation point of the Iberian treasure fleets sailing for Europe. Here was the gathering place for the bulk of gold and silver taken from citizens and mines of North America. The storm had blown the Englishmen from the Yucatan channel into the Gulf of Campeche.

All published records of this time must be considered suspect, be they Spanish or English. As has already been stated, North America was a prize all Europe wanted and political intrigue was an undercurrent in every written and published document. Strict censorship was imposed on all English and Spanish publications by their respective countries, so when the record states that John Hawkins' fleet had to go into San Juan de Ulloa for "needed repairs," the statement should be looked upon with some scrutiny. The decrepit old *Jesus* may have truly been leaking to an extreme, but the necessity of going into San Juan de Ulloa may have been used as an excuse to engage in spying activities.

Inside the shallow, cramped harbor were twelve loaded treasure galleons, all with little or no armament. Hawkins sailed in with two warships and four cargo vessels thus creating a situation of high tension among both Spaniards and Englishmen. It is said that the Spanish were taken by surprise when the British arrived, as they were expecting an escort fleet for the treasure ships and assumed the arriving group was it. This could well be so, as the Iberians had probably never seen the escort fleet before, thus would have had no way to recognize it. It is extremely doubtful, however, that there were any surprises for John Hawkins. Not even the most naïve English sailor would boldly slide into the main port of the opposition without first reconnoitering the area. Hawkins was, to say the least, not naïve. He was instead a smart and bold trader who on that trip was backed by two warships.

Yet, just before arriving at San Juan, Hawkins had overhauled three small passenger ships and took on one hundred people as hostages. Having a warship in danger of sinking, but stopping to accost three vessels and take that many hostages does not add up to a linear continuity of events. Perhaps John Hawkins knew the plate fleet was in the harbor and that the large number of hostages could guarantee peaceful trading regarding the western hemisphere silver and gold. Of course, the guns of the *Jesus* and the *Minion* would guarantee the English would receive a fair price. As even a Spanish doubloon must have two sides, it was Hawkins' turn to be surprised when the flip side of Lady Luck's coin turned over for him. No sooner had his fleet been securely moored to the quay with their stern anchors run out, when the Spanish escort flotilla sailed into sight, prepared to defend the treasure ships. Hawkins' position by then was not an enviable one. Not only were his vessels tied bow-on to the stone quay with no chance to make a run for it, but even if they had been pointed out to sea, there would have been little chance for escape from the narrow-mouthed harbor.

Consternation of their position quieted somewhat when the English realized they were not the only ones in a trap. Perhaps the situation was one of equal concern for both factions, similar to a "Mexican Standoff," with peril on both sides. The Spanish escort fleet was in a dangerous way, for it was the beginning of hurricane season and to be caught this close to shore by one of those shrieking gales could well send the entire flotilla to the bottom, scattering their planks and personnel high on the mainland beaches.

John Hawkins realized he was the underdog in this game of marine chess and it was important for him to make a move, and a fast one. His queen had forbid him to enter into any fireplay with ships or personnel of his Royal Spanish Majesty. To do so would place the English crown in an extremely bad political position, indeed one that could lead to war; something gold-poor England could not afford. Bluster, bravado and bluff were the only chance for the British "traders," and not too much time could be spent orchestrating that game, for a delay might see the Spanish caught in a ship-wrecking storm. Hawkins knew too well that if this were allowed to come to pass, it too would mean political jeopardy for Elizabeth and all the rest at home.

Bargaining began back and forth between the two groups. With twelve Spanish ships inside the harbor and thirteen outside at sea, John Hawkins was not happy with his options, no matter how the situation would evolve. Perhaps it was necessity and love of profit for the English that consummated an agreement for the outlying Spanish ships to come into the harbor, with the allowance for Hawkins to stay and repair his vessels and thence do necessary trading for supplies. Nothing is recorded about the hostages who apparently were turned free to go ashore.

Thirteen Spanish ships under the command of Don Francisco de Luxan sailed into the already crowded little cove and tied up close to the English traders. There were by then twenty-five Spanish hulls and six English bottoms in the harbor of San Juan de Ulloa, hardly odds that even Drake could ignore.

In spite of all agreements, the two sides were soon at each other's throats. It is not hard to imagine a British sailor taunting the crew on an opposing ship with a statement such as, "The odds are about even. One Englishman to ten Spaniards!" And some hot-blooded Iberian yelling back, "Tell us when you're ready and we'll draw and quarter the lot of you mutton-eating heretics!"

It is impossible to ascertain from sketchy records the exact reason for breaking the fragile truce. Each commander blamed the other. Guns were soon bellowing through clouds of acrid black powder smoke. Masts and heavy spars came crashing to the decks of vessels, carrying with them massive tangles of lines. Large splinters of wood blasted from bulwarks, small boats, above-deck cabins and other upper parts of the vessels, and the debris hummed through the air as chain shot and ball tore at the ships. In the small, cramped moorage amidst the flying rubble, smoke and thundering roar, with men from both sides running in all directions, the fantastic confusion must have been unlike any other "sea" battle in history.

With keen enjoyment, the Spanish told how the "Devil Drake" was forced to leap into the bay, thence swim to the *Judith* where he hauled himself aboard hand over hand, along a slack mooring line. Possibly the daring English seaman had found it expedient to cut the *Judith's* line free from the dockside and the small vessel, already with some canvas up, sharply swung away from the pier before Drake could leap back aboard his ship. The old *Jesus* was doomed. Already badly strained from the storm before entering the harbor, the larger of the English gunships drew the bulk of the fire from the Spanish. Contrary to the embellished and biased statements of some historians, nationality has nothing to do with the degree of a sailor's ability. Some fine gunners on Spanish decks were making scrap wood out of the upperworks of the large British ship.

Meanwhile, a wind was fast picking up and Francis Drake had managed to get the maneuverable little *Judith* underway. The *Minion* had fared much better than her larger counterpart, *Jesus*, because her skipper was a man of quick action. As soon as the guns started bellowing, he had part of his crew at a capstan hauling in on the stern anchor line to kedge the *Minion* stern-first into the channel while others raced to the bow to cut mooring lines. At the same time, all guns on the side facing the Spanish fired steadily. As she slipped alongside and past the badly battered hulk of the *Jesus*, Hawkins and those of his crew able to do so, abandoned the old flagship and clambered aboard the smaller vessel.

Left behind in the harbor were the riddle hulls of the *Jesus*, *Swallow*, *Angel*, and the captured Portuguese hull, *Grace of God*. Also lost to the Spanish for capture were many English seamen.

The Spanish fared worse than their adversaries. Of the escort flotilla, four ships were sunk, constituting a greater loss in tonnage than that of the English. Also, later reports indicated that more than five hundred Spaniards were killed.

After having made it out of the harbor and into the open sea, strong winds separated the *Minion* and the *Judith*. Drake sailed the *Judith* into Plymouth Harbor on January 20, 1569. Five days later, Hawkins arrived at Mount's Bay in Cornwall with the *Minion*. The *William and John* had also escaped from San Juan de Ulloa and made port.

John Hawkins subsequently wrote an account of the events. In the record attributed to him it states, "So with the *Minion* only and the *Judith* (a small barke of fifty tunne) we escaped, which barke the same night forstoke us in our great miserie."

Many historical writers have tried to make out from this statement that Drake had deserted his commander. These same writers should be blessed with the experience of being on a small vessel in a hard blow. Their pens would quickly skip over making anyone out a coward in those conditions. Even when a cockleshell of fifty tons is well found, a hard blow renders it completely helpless, being unable to do anything other than ride it out until the wind dies down. Both the *Minion* and the *Judith* could not have escaped the battle without some damage, and both were overcrowded with men. Add a storm and wounded seamen to the conditions of the ships and it becomes a small miracle that either vessel arrived back home. There was no such thing as one vessel deserting the other. Separation during the night in hurricane winds would have been inevitable. In the face of all the conditions, including being in enemy waters, the prudent choice for either captain would be to get the hell out of there as fast as he could. That the *Minion* arrived in Plymouth only five days after Drake and the *Judith* is ample proof that both captains, by agreement, headed their ships for home immediately after leaving San Juan de Ulloa. John Hawkins was too good a sailor to have meant to degrade Francis Drake. Methinks he had his tongue in cheek when he said the fifty-tonner "forsooke" the three-hundred-tonner.

GOLDEN HINDE

CHAPTER 5

ALMOST SIXTEEN MONTHS had passed since the ill-fated six had braced their yards for the English Channel and out of Plymouth Harbor. The religious situation in the isles was becoming more intense and hostile, if such a thing were possible. On the political front, a new and explosive situation had evolved.

Two months before the return of Francis Drake and the *Judith*, several ships of Spain had put into Plymouth Harbor seeking refuge from French privateers who had been "hot on their transoms." The ships apparently reached port just in the nick of time. As events turned out, however, they may have been better off to have tried fighting or out-sailing the pirates. On board the Iberian ships was gold bullion amounting to a hundred thousand pounds. This gold was destined to go to Duke of Alva, the Spanish governor of the Netherlands, since that country was then under the yoke of Spain. The gold was needed to pay Alva's army.

Don Guerau de Spes, the Spanish ambassador to England, hit upon a scheme designed to outwit the French corsairs hovering near the entrance to Plymouth Harbor. He asked Queen Elizabeth for safe conduct to be given the bullion as it was transshipped overland from Plymouth to Dover, where he intended to put it aboard ship again for a fast dash across the channel to the Netherlands.

However, gold-poor England, headed by Europe's best

profit-scheming sovereign, was not a combination the ambassador should have tried to deal with. Elizabeth not only abhorred seeing funds escape her needy government's coffers, but if Alva's army was to receive the bullion, it directly increased their threat to England. Queen Bess stalled for time. She informed ambassador Don Guerau that she did not wish to deprive the Dutch merchants of any part of the money for Spanish military purchases, but that it was detrimental to the English for any monies to reach Alva's army.

While the enraged Don Guerau de Spes furiously endeavored to get his request granted, his homeland learned of the situation and proceeded to ask the English ambassador at Madrid to withdraw from the court. Prompt retaliation for this treatment of her emissary caused Elizabeth to place the Spanish ambassador under arrest in his home.

It was at this time that the little fifty-ton bark with its overload of adventurous mariners and their bold captain arrived in port. Francis Drake's sailing into the same harbor where Spanish bullion ships were tied up must have caused a furor. Many of Drake's crew were wounded and some had died on the way home. It has been recorded that the survivors had little food or water on their return trip, so this half-starved, worn out group of sailors arriving at their home port in their little shot-up vessel, all the result of Spanish action, further divided the good relations between the Spanish and English.

Francis Drake was ordered to report to the Crown Council immediately. His story of the ill-fated adventure was barely told when the leader of the expedition, cousin John Hawkins, arrived sea-worn to add his words to the record. Any hopes Don Guerau and the crown of Spain may have had for the transshipping of the cargo of bullion were scuttled. By the queen's order, the gold was ensconced in the Tower of London for "safety."

Hawkins' tale of the San Juan de Ulloa fight and its results markedly changed the thinking of many in the Crown Council. Several of those who had been pressing for friendly trade relations with Spain at any cost began to doubt the wisdom of this course.

San Juan de Ulloa and the confiscation of Philip's gold created bow-string tensions between England and Spain as the two charged and counter-charged each other with accusations ranging from misconduct to war-like behavior. Trade between the two nations came to a standstill as a result of each placing commerce embargos upon the other.

At this point, Francis Drake joined the navy. Quite probably his actions at San Juan brought forth the offer of fast advancement in the service, if he would enlist. This decision was another important step toward his greatness as a mariner.

On July 4th in the summer of 1569, while on leave from the service, Francis Drake married Mary Newman of St. Budeaux, near the town of Plymouth. Almost nothing is known of this union. Perhaps it was of short duration, for only the staunchest of women can stand up to the innumerable tests that come of being married to a man who has succumbed to the irresistible need for the feel of a surging deck beneath his feet. Some men thrive when screaming winds and thundering water threaten to wash him into the cold, black depths. The sea is also a persuasive beckoning hand, always promising a glass-like surface and lazy warm days with moonlit nights of solitude that allow complete absorption in one's own thoughts, the only interruption being the muffled groan of a protesting ship's joint as two hull timbers move ever so slightly against each other.

In a storm, the seaman cusses the day he had been so ignorant as to leave the land. He swears to his maker that if He will just let him get through this blow alive, the ocean will never see him again. But ashore once again with a shining sun and watching a vessel leave port until it is hull-down on the horizon, is another story. The press of land with its stream of bills calling for attention and the endless obligations from hordes of humanity erases the memory of storms and cold. Only the beauty of the sea has a place in the mind. Once more the sailor runs away to the tranquility of solitude. He ships out once again. Forgotten is his promise to the Almighty, and the Overseer forgives the forgetfulness.

Francis Drake married and went back to sea. There were no offspring resulting from his union with Mary Newman.

CHAPTER 6

THE REFORMATION IN England was then facing one of its most crucial tests. A move was afoot to release Mary Stuart, Queen of Scots, from her prison. Catholics in the north were on the verge of insurrection. England was busily engaged in preparations for war that might come from any side, or from within. The French were a threat, but conflict came from the north as the Catholics rebelled. The insurrection was fortunately quickly quelled as the Duke of Alva was preparing to take advantage of the revolt by attacking England from the Netherlands. Prudence overshadowed valor when the Duke decided to refrain from involvement with the islanders.

While Drake was adjusting to both married and navy life, cousin John Hawkins was busily engaged in assembling a fleet of twelve ships for an unknown venture. The Spanish ambassador was alarmed at the proceedings, and notified his king that Hawkins was possibly preparing to avenge the affair at San Juan de Ulloa. Immediate preparations were taken to repulse such an effort, with messages of warning sent to all Spanish ports. The ambassador's fears were unfounded. With the French threat and possible invasion by Alva, all English ships were pressed into the needs of the navy. Hawkins' preparations came to an end.

Although Spain's Duke of Alva prepared for an invasion of England and Elizabeth the "Navy Queen" prepared her fleet to repulse, neither party was adequately ready for a sea war. Spain had few vessels that could be termed fighting ships, and England's navy had badly deteriorated due to the press of more needful expenditures. Elizabeth's navy, most of which she had inherited from her father, was not in good enough shape to engage an enemy with any guarantee of success. The queen knew this. Her shrewdness for profit, coupled with the wisdom of many in her council, induced a cold war designed to gain for trade-poor Britain a place of power in the world. The policy of "no open conflict" was continued, the same policy that resulted in so much difficulty for John Hawkins and Francis Drake at San Juan.

New Spain was a land of mystery to all of Europe except the Spanish who occupied the mysterious country. Conflicting stories by seamen who had served on Spanish ships confused and obscured information concerning the country that bounded on the Caribbean Sea. Some said it was a desolate, heat-ridden, mosquito-infested land that offered little in the way of ports; a place poorly defended by the Spanish.

Others, divested of information by way of plied drink or coin, asserted that New Spain was a land of riches, with gold and silver in every handful of earth. They said it was a place of fine harbors, protected by impregnable forts manned by thousands of Spanish dragoons.

The English had little doubt that the new land had great riches and that Spain was guarding it with all her resources. The deadly international game of intrigue continually revealed truths, myths, and lies. The never-ending chore of separating fact from fantasy in the tales created only increased confusion for the Queen's Council.

The treasure-loaded vessels of the Iberians could not be denied. Hawkins had proven that at least some of the Spanish ports in the Gulf of Mexico were not well defended, but there were others of which very little was known. If the English Crown were to make a move to gain advantageous footholds in North America, then more firsthand knowledge of the coasts had to be sought and gained.

Small local and coastal trading vessels of numerous types

continually came and went through the harbor waters of Plymouth. Scarce attention was paid to this type of traffic, for seldom was any personage or cargo important enough to alert the espionage system of Spain. Therefore, little note was made when two small sails slipped out of the harbor in 1570. The vessels were the *Dragon* and the *Swan*. The hulls may have been too small for the Spanish spies to pay them heed, but the man in charge was of importance.

Francis Drake was commanding his first foray against Spain. The "English Devil" had sustained nothing but losses on his other voyages to the West Indies, but this time he would not be a subordinate officer; instead, his would be the word to follow. Of this marine incursion, almost nothing is known. The same amount of record is available for a following voyage in 1571 when the stocky mariner made a similar trip with only the *Swan*.

Most historians suspect that Drake was on probes of exploration in 1570 and 1571. They are probably correct. Drake joined the navy in 1569 and records show him to be in the Queen's service in 1579 while on the west coast of the Americas during his voyage of circumnavigation, and again when contributing to the defeat of the Spanish Armada in 1588. There can be little doubt that Francis Drake was continually in the service of his country, whenever at sea, from 1569 until his death in 1596.

At the time of the departure of the *Dragon* and the *Swan*, Spain had occupied the mainland of North America for more than three decades. It was known by the English that the west coast of South America produced large quantities of gold and silver. Reports had also trickled back to Europe of considerable high-profit mining to the north of Mexico City.

By then also, sailor's yarns, bandied about in European ports, insisted that the Spanish were voyaging far to the north on the west coast of North America. It was whispered that regardless of what the politicos had to say, the Straits of Anian had been discovered. Some said a Portuguese by the name of Juan Cabrillo had discovered the straights, but that ice and extreme cold had turned him back. There were also those who discounted the discovery of the straits. They stated

Cabrillo had reached only 43 degrees north latitude and that was where he died, buried on a lonely, desolate island. There were still other reports that said French fishermen, coming from the Straits of Ballacas at the mouth of the great inland North American lakes on the east side of the new continent, had heard by way of Indians that the Spanish were far in the north and opposite the coast of Labrador.

The Drake voyages of 1570 and 1571 were quite probably spy missions into the Caribbean solely for the purpose of learning the location of Spanish ports, the Iberian methods regarding transport of gold and silver, and any other information that might be deemed important to the general welfare of his homeland.

To bring an accurate focus to the activities of Spain and England on the coast of America at that time a comparison of the two nations needs to be drawn. Spain had been a world leader in sea exploration for many decades before the English nation had been aroused to the necessity for expansion. By the time Francis Drake made his trip with the vessels the *Dragon* and the *Swan*, the riches of North and South America had been discovered and the Spanish had succumbed to gold and silver fever.

Spanish explorers had already discovered a commercially-strategic piece of ground—the Isthmus of Panama—and they had the narrow strip of land well under their control. For many years, Spain's small coastal vessels had been trading up and down the coast of the Caribbean, obtaining useful and exotic products for the motherland. All of the small ports were well known. Most of those, at least the ones of importance, contained a town governed by Spain in which the Catholic religion was well established. The Spanish Caribbean natives had, in fact, a well-ordered way of life with the daily chores of living only slightly interrupted by the occupation of the European conquerors.

Vera Cruz was the center of activity on the east coast of the isthmus. There, the slow way of life in the tropics was occasionally interrupted by excitement when mule trains arrived with gold and silver bullion from the Pacific Coast and inland mountain areas. Vera Cruz was the port of call for ships arriving from Spain. The primary thought in the minds of all people arriving at this harbor was the strong possibility of gaining immediate wealth.

Spanish exploration activity was by then concentrated to the north of Mexico. Both marine and land expeditions were continually readied for penetration into the unknown areas of New Spain. From their homeland in Europe, thousands of soldiers and sailors arrived on the Vera Cruz shore each year to try their hand at becoming prosperous conquistadors.

The English were just as excited as their Spanish adversaries when it came to mineral wealth, but with Spain's tight hold on the isthmus, the easy door to the wealth of North America was effectively barred.

Englishmen of knowledge, from Queen Elizabeth on down to the man in the fo'castle, knew that it would be difficult for Britishers to obtain a significant share of the western world. Possession of land and wealth would have to be gained methodically, one difficult step at a time. Elizabeth I and her privy council set forth to establish an empire. Perhaps this red-haired monarch deserves to be labeled the first of a long line of "English Bulldogs."

It can be surmised that Drake, with the little vessels the *Swan* and the *Dragon*, slowly and surreptitiously made his way carefully along the Gulf Coast, drawing profiles of the shoreline and carefully taking bearings on prominent peaks. He also recorded their latitudes for use by future voyaging countrymen. Harbors may have been entered in a small pull boat with the lead being methodically heaved ahead to measure and record the depths for England's subsequent trading and exploration vessels.

The seamen of the Mediterranean must be given credit for first exploitation of scientific navigational practices. Prince Henry of Portugal, known as Henry the Navigator, taught the track of the sea by using a huge compass laid out on the ground employing rows of stone. It was a Spanish school of navigation that taught an Englishman a better method of piloting, which inspired him to set up a similar institution of learning in his homeland.

Advances in navigational practices slowed almost to a

halt in Spain in the sixteenth century. Perhaps it was because the long tracks on the seas of the world had been tried, and the mariners were too busy lining their pockets in the new lands to worry much about navigational improvement. The track of Columbus had become a well-scoured trough in the 1600s, and Magellan's groove in the Pacific was proven again and again by Portuguese and Spanish pilots. The "tried and true" method of sailing on the latitude, with the use of the pegboard for checking distance and course, was good enough for the Iberians. Like most seamen of any age, they preferred the absence of any radical change that might tax their minds beyond what they considered their capacity. The use of the lookout was an unfailing method of ascertaining the proximity of the shore. If the sailor could not see a danger, and the weather was clear, then why worry about the fine points of longitude and latitude? If the weather was bad, with no visibility due to night rain or fog, then the prudent navigator simply reefed his sails and sat it out. Of course, many vessels were lost, but there was always another ship and another crew.

Vessels crossed as little open water out of the sight of land, as possible. It was the practice to run along the coast, from cape to cape, for hundreds of miles rather than to risk a crossing where shore could no longer be seen.

To the English must go the credit for scientific tracking of the seas of the world. It is perhaps misleading to state that Queen Elizabeth I was the primary driving power that began the acceleration of nautical science, but most certainly it was during her time that England surged forward in this monumental effort, which eventually gave that nation control of the seas. Many men of Tudor times contributed to better and more exacting methods of charting the oceans, surveying the land, and measuring the breadth of entire continents.

When in 1571 Drake again made a voyage to the Indies, it was with only one vessel, the *Swan*. Extremely small—she was only thirty tons—the little bark had probably proven to handle well on the previous trip the year before and perhaps had a shallower draft than the *Dragon*. Scholars have speculated that this voyage was one of reconnaissance, but there is faint record regarding the trip's purpose. Perhaps the secret files of the British government have charts made by Drake during this foray, but for the public there is no record available.

The ensuing year, and another voyage, at least partly told the tale of the two "exploration" trips of 1570 and 1571. One Whitsunday evening, May 24, 1572, the *Swan* sailed out of the Plymouth sound and once again headed for Spanish water to the west. With it this time was a ship almost three times the size of the little veteran. Ship *Pasha* was commanded by Captain Drake, the "Admiral" of the new and daring two-sail fleet. It is the deficient, but important, chronicles of the 1572 voyage that cast some dim light onto the operations of the previous two.

While slipping about the Spanish Main in the *Swan*, Drake had discovered a small, secluded cove on the Darian coast where he realized a few small vessels could remain relatively well hidden from Spanish mariner's eyes. The finding of the little port brought about the beginning glimmers of an idea by which he could relieve the Iberians of a small part of their ill-gotten metallic wealth.

GOLDEN HINDE

CHAPTER 7

Drake the "Devil" was now starting to live up to the nickname given him by the Spanish who hated him. Drake's burning need to recoup his financial losses received at Rio de la Hacha and San Juan de Ulloa was an ever-present, all-consuming feeling within the young sea dog. Since the first theft of profits, when Miguel de Castellanos marched off with Drake's share of the slaves, a multitude of plans for revenge had been nurtured. Most of the plans had been discarded as unsound.

One plan, long dreamed of, was to boldly attack King Philip's treasure house at Nombre de Dios, the eastern terminal of the mule trail across the Isthmus of Panama. The silver and gold from south Central America and northwest South American mines was stored there while it awaited shipment across the Atlantic to Spain where it would finance the powerful nation's European activities.

To dream of sacking the Spanish treasure house was one thing; to carry out such a magnificent undertaking was quite something different. The San Juan del Ulloa experience had most certainly taught the mariner that to sail right up to the Iberian's door was not the most intelligent of plans, for this same exploit had taught that one could well be painfully surprised by unexpected visitors. No, to carry out such a bold mission on Nombre de Dios, the operation must be one of an entirely different nature than had ever been attempted before.

Port Pheasant, as Francis Drake had named the hidden cove because many such birds were breeding there, furnished the key to the new plan for shrinking Spain's pocketbook. To arrive at a Spanish harbor in ships and then sack it would mean that within a few days a fleet of well-armed warships would arrive searching for the invaders. Odds were they might be caught and at least part of the company and its vessels lost. To raid the Spanish was not only great sport, it was also a business venture. And the possibility of losing men and ships did not augur a profitable enterprise. Any overland attack was also of dubious execution, for much of the country was swampland. Before a company could return to their ships moored nearby, the Spaniards could conceivably have arrived at the anchorage and either captured or sunk the English vessels. Then, the raiders, caught on shore, would be at the mercy of the Spaniards.

Port Pheasant offered a new way of attack on the Iberians. There, a camp could be established in a haven well suited for small boats, but too shallow and confined for large vessels. The discovery of this bit of secluded coastal geography eventually generated a bold plan in the mind of Francis Drake.

On July 12th, the *Swan* and the *Pasha* arrived off the entrance of Port Pheasant. The jolly boat of the *Pasha* was swung out over the side. Drake and a seaman dropped into it and rowed for the narrow entrance of the secret cove.

When the two ships had hove-to at the mouth of the bay, they had noticed smoke coming from somewhere on the nearby shore, which is why it was deemed prudent to ease warily into the lagoon by dinghy and see who tended the fire. This was not to be accomplished so easily for Drake and his seaman soon found the smoke to be rising from within the jungle a short distance from the cove beach. There was no way to ascertain who had built the fire, nor how many persons were at its location. A hard pull with one oar, and a deep push with the other spun the little jolly boat on its short keel. Drake and his man headed back to the *Swan* and *Pasha* for reinforcements.

Men scrambled into the ship's boats, loaded their

firearms, and then quickly pulled towards the beach at Port Pheasant. Only the raucous screeches of jungle birds and the faint pleasant aroma of wood smoke greeted them as they jumped ashore at the ready. Cautiously and quietly the sailors moved into the dense undergrowth in the direction of the smoke. It was only a few dozen steps before they discovered a smoldering log with no humans to be seen anywhere in the area.

Near the slowly burning timber was a little sapling with a small piece of sheet lead fastened to it. On the metal was scratched a message to Drake, telling him the Spanish knew of this cove and that they had found some stores he had hidden there on the previous voyage with the *Swan*. (Sheet lead had many advantages for writing messages, for it was easily inscribed and would not deteriorate quickly in the weather.) The message was signed by John Garrett.

Little is known of Garrett, other than he was an English privateer and that possibly he had some men with him who had previously sailed with Drake. Sailors routinely changed from ship to ship in the sixteenth century, just as they do today. "Friend" Garrett may well have been the one who rifled Drake's cache, only to conveniently blame it on the common enemy. Drake apparently thought this, or at least considered it a possibility, because he carried on with his plans although he must have altered them a bit.

The pull boats towed the *Swan* and the *Pasha* through the narrow rocky bay entrance to the protected anchorage inside.

From Plymouth had been brought three knocked-down small pinnaces. These small sailing tenders were the key to Drake's new method of attack on the Spanish. With them he intended to steal up the coast under cover of darkness, then land near the bullion terminal of Nombre de Dios. The plan was that the Spanish, not seeing any hulls or masts on the sea, would assume the attack had been perpetrated by a band trekking some distance over land. Then, while confusion reigned, Drake and his men could withdraw in the pinnaces, sail back to Port Pheasant still under the concealing shroud of night, and the Spanish would be at a loss to understand how the raid had been executed.

Planks and pre-steamed ribs of the pinnaces were brought ashore and a construction "jig" was set up to speed their assembly. While this operation took place, a log fort or breastwork was built for protection if, by chance, there were some armed Spaniards in the area who might take umbrage to the English for being there and thus attack. Spaniards were not a great worry to Drake, except that the message of Garrett warranted caution. Normally, the only people who might be in the area were natives and Cimarrones. "Cimarrones" were escaped black slaves of the Spanish. There was little to be feared of these people, as they wanted little to do with Europeans.

Around the log fort a large, wide swath was cleared of jungle growth to furnish open space an attacker would have to cross in order to get to the breastwork, thus furnishing those in the crude stronghold a chance to shoot at an exposed target.

Scarcely had the pinnace frames been set up and the construction of the fort started, that the lookout at the cover entrance warned the group of approaching ships. It seemed as though the raiding operation might be doomed before it had gotten under way.

Considerable relief was felt when the intruding group of vessels proved to be led by a ship belonging to Sir Edward Horsey and commanded by the English privateer James Ranse. During the San Juan de Ulloa engagement, the ship *William and John* had been commanded by a James Ranse and there is little doubt that the new arrival at Port Pheasant was one and the same.

The appearance of Ranse was conceivably both a blessing and a hindrance to Drake's plans. The new arrivals would significantly add manpower to the venture, providing better chance of success by way of force. Detrimentally though, more troops meant proportionately greater hazards by means of added confusion, which in turn could create less control over the group. True, another leader had also been joined into the venture, but this could also be a loss instead of a gain. A man such as Ranse, who was more accustomed to giving orders than taking them, could quite easily constitute the downfall of the expedition simply by following his nature and giving an apparently unimportant order to the men at a time when Drake or his lieutenants were not in the vicinity. The bulk of Drake's men would follow a Ranse directive, some probably having sailed under him at an earlier time. Even though James Ranse might issue a directive, one that on the surface could well be plausible, it is just this type of incident that have caused more than a few bold undertakings to fail.

An operation such as Drake's assault on the Spanish treasure depository must well be thought out and planned in advance. Every movement of supplies, men, ships and arms needs to be patterned well ahead if the completed mission is to be successful. When planning a secret or dangerous task, the fewer people who are cognizant of the details, the better the chances are of favorable termination.

Undoubtedly, Francis Drake had planned and re-planned this voyage for many months, possibly several years, until he felt all risks had been minimized. Just as surely, he had not disclosed his scheme in detail to more people than absolutely necessary. Unquestionably, he had told his crew as little as possible when signing them on the ship's papers, for sailors are prone to gab and waterfront news has a way of traveling from one end of a harbor's dockline to the other in a matter of a few short minutes.

It was the combination of this necessary secrecy and Captain James Ranse turning up on the scene at a most inopportune time that placed the success of the campaign in jeopardy. Drake recognized the possible risks involved, but there was little he could do. A countryman, who apparently had been with him on other ventures, joined his group. Naturally, Ranse would expect Drake to invite him to join in on any scheme, or perhaps they could devise one together.

There was nothing Drake could do but to outwardly appear overjoyed at the appearance of the privateer when he hove-to off the entrance of Port Pheasant. It was a case of just hoping for the best. Beyond question, Drake informed Captain Ranse, just as graciously as circumstance permitted, that this was a Drake operation and that long-laid plans had been made and must be followed. Doubtless, Ranse agreed with sincerity, but the ingredient of possible disruption remained.

To secure himself as much protection as obtainable, Drake proceeded to draw up a document that was signed by both captains. The document included a statement wherein the shares of spoils were agreed upon and leadership specifically stated. Drake had made the best of a position brought about by an unforeseen circumstance.

Quite possibly, Captain Ranse's arrival, or the inscribed lead plate and burning log left by John Garrett, created a change in plans regarding the ships. In the beginning, Drake may have planned to hide his vessels in the little cove of Port Pheasant while he slipped up the coast in the pinnaces. He may have decided that the Spanish were well aware of his base and could get to it before he could up-anchor after the assault on Nombre de Dios, or that with Ranse's additional hulls there would not be enough room to hide all the vessels' masts from a watchful Spanish squadron. Regardless of what the reason was, Drake resolved to move the fleet to another hiding place.

The three pinnaces had by then, after a week's assembly, been christened the *Minion*, *Eion*, and *Lion*. With these small boats trailing in the wakes, the fleet and adventurers sailed northwest up the Darian coast where they arrived at small fir-clad islands. The "Isles of Pines," as they were dubbed, furnished another surprise and obstacle to the expedition's leader. At the beach, in a narrow channel between the islands, were a few Negro slaves loading planks and timbers onto two small frigates.

Although other works written of this incident simply state there were two vessels and Negro slaves, one cannot help but think there must have been a few Spanish guards overseeing the operation. Most certainly, black slaves would not be allowed to have two frigates completely under their control. This author believes it would be safe to surmise that the adventurers eliminated some possible Spanish intervention.

In one sense, the timber loaders were an asset because information about Nombre de Dios was badly needed. Drake found that the slaves were stowing the timber for use in the Spanish city. This meant a bad break had resolved itself into an incident of possible good fortune. Interrogation of the black men brought forth the information that an added detachment of Spanish soldiers was due to arrive in Madre de Dios very soon. Also, the Cimarrones were in revolt. The additional troops being brought in to counter the Cimarrones' threat would also be an additional hazard to Drake's attack.

Spanish policy toward conquered peoples in the new world was one of many conflicting projections. Each group of conquerors had their own methods of dealing with natives. Cruelty, hard labor, poor food and little of it, and with almost no rights whatsoever, was the lot of the Aztecs and other Indian tribes. Imported slaves from Africa had an even harder life than that of the Indians, if that is possible. Representatives of the Catholic Church, such as the Jesuits, Franciscans, Carmelites, Dominicans and so forth, earnestly tried to better the lot of the Indian by teaching him European crafts. But these religious missionaries had an obligation not only to the church, but also the Spanish crown, thus much cruelty of the Indians was accepted by the "Padres" in order that they might continue teaching the Catholic faith to the natives.

The Spanish crown advocated gentle and kind treatment of conquered people. In fact, over and over, on document after document originating from the crown, orders specifying this position were sent to the political leaders of Mexico and New Spain. There was yet another element though that had to be reckoned with, an element that all—Crown, religious clergy and colonizers—had to put up with, for without them none would be in this rich land. That element was the soldier, the "Conquistador" as he was then known.

The monarchy of Spain wanted gold. The people of Europe wanted products from Central America with which they could have a better life. The Vatican wanted more converts to the Catholic religion. None of these desires could be accomplished without the efforts of the Conquistador. To obtain more gold and silver, more and more slaves were needed. If a native objected to being used, he might be flayed until the meat was stripped from his bones. It was a blessing if he died quickly. If there was no time for a flogging, the objecting Indian might simply be run through with a pike and left to die a long, slow, agonizing death with no one allowed to give the injured one succor of any kind. The Church protested. The king protested, but only to a degree that did not hamper the Conquistador in his efforts to conquer more lands for the other two groups to enjoy.

It should be noted that a "mere whipping," such as a few lashes with a "blacksnake" was not considered cruel. The transgression of a minor Spanish rule or law was just cause for any Spanish official, high or unimportant, to order a whipping. Even the Padre in charge of a mission believed it just cause to lash a convert who did not obey the will of the church's envoy. Suffering the most oppression was the black man. He was an import to the new land and a minority in numbers. It was not considered important to the religious to convert a black man nor teach him, so he was generally ignored. Thus, he also lacked even the smallest amount of protective voice occasionally uttered by the church and sovereignty on behalf of the Indians.

Indian slave labor was not good enough for the Spanish. The natives were lazy and rebellious. They were continually causing problems and staging small uprisings. On the other hand, the imported African Negro was far different. He endured hard work with a minimum of oversight and accepted the rigorous life with little protest.

The Cimarrones were a different breed of people than the black or the Indian. In fact, the Cimarrones were a combination of the two races. This blending of peoples produced a race that was quite willing to fight the Spanish. So willing, in fact, that it was these independent people who caused the Iberians to send another detachment of soldiers to Nombre de Dios. Although a quite hardy folk, even some of the Africans could not endure the Spanish treatment and many ran off into the Mexican and Central American jungle. It was their offspring, from their junction with Aztec women that produced the Cimarrone.

Francis Drake was known through his life as a tolerant

man who endeavored to treat all people, regardless of race, with respect. A strange facet of this great mariner is that he was quite able to participate in the endeavor of securing and selling slaves to the Spanish even when he knew of the life ahead for them. There is the very real possibility that he considered their new life to be no worse than the one endured in their native Africa. Too, he may have felt that if he didn't participate in this lucrative enterprise, there was always someone else willing to take his place and his abstinence would gain nothing. African slaving was simply an accepted part of the times.

After interrogating the blacks at the Isles of Pines, the problem of keeping them silent about his arrival in the area became one of highest importance. Questioning had revealed the welcome news that the Spanish had no knowledge of his being in the Caribbean.

A solution of simplicity evolved from discussions concerning the Negroes. The black men would be set ashore on the mainland, just before the expedition set out for Nombre de Dios. There was no way to travel fast through the jungle of this land of Darian because of the dense growth and quagmires. So, if there might be one of the blacks inclined to report to the Spanish about the presence of Drake and his expedition, the man would not be able to reach Nombre de Dios before the Englishmen had accomplished their objective. Perhaps some of the blacks had expressed their desire to join the jungle tribes and the Cimarrones.

It was at the end of July when the three pinnaces, loaded with fifty-three of Drake's men, and Ranse's longboat carrying twenty of his crew, threaded their way out of the narrows between the Isles of Pines. Captain Ranse was left behind in charge of his vessel and the captured hulls, Drake's ships, and the two newly captured Spanish frigates. If danger had existed before from a possible double command, it was now effectively and conveniently eliminated for certainly a reliable leader was needed to be in charge of the hidden fleet and escape vehicles for the returning raiding party.

Cautiously the little armada of pull/sail boats, bristling with men and guns, worked its way northwest up the mainland coast. Sails were used when possible, but only when a cautious watch was kept both seaward and landward, for a mast and sail is considerably more easily spotted than a boat propelled by oars. A longboat disappears from sight much of the time as it sinks into the hollow between swells when traveling along a coast, especially if there is a "good sea running." It requires only swells a few feet high to conceal the hull of a small vessel from a beach watcher. Put a mast and sail on the same hull and it is seldom completely out of view.

Traveling close along the coast was executed only in the darkest hours of night. After five days, the little flotilla had moved approximately twenty-five leagues from the ship anchorage. They arrived at a small island during the shadowy hours of dawn. Here the arms, consisting of targets (shields), pikes, fire pikes, muskets, calivers, bows, swords, and partisans were served out. The day was spent in training for the assault, the men drilled over and over on the method of approach that would be used when entering Nombre de Dios, and the plan of attack that would be followed once the landing was made.

At dusk, the boats were again entered and their stems pointed toward the Spanish port. The plan was to arrive in the dark hours at the mouth of the Rio San Francisco, a small river close to Nombre de Dios, then, when sufficient light of the beginning dawn would allow the men to attack and fight, the town would be entered.

It seemed that fortune was to shine on the corsairs as the glow of the rising moon brought sufficient light a good hour before dawn. An advantage surely, for the town and its guard of soldiers would be still in slumber. With oars muffled by clothing wrapped around them and the locks, the boats with silent crews quietly glided toward the harbor quays.

Once more it would appear as though fortune had reversed itself on Drake. As the pinnaces and longboat rounded the harbor point, they abruptly came into view of a Spanish ship's boat crew pulling towards the shore from a wine-laden freight vessel that had only hours before arrived in the port.

It was not a time for a hesitant man to make decisions. As quickly as the Spaniards were sighted, Drake gave the order for his boats to head off the Iberians. It could not be allowed that they arrive ashore first to spread the alarm. So, the English boats surged ahead.

Cut off, the unarmed Spanish sailors were quick to see the wisdom of obeying the order to go elsewhere and remain detached from the coming events. After all, they were working a merchant vessel transporting wine and when they signed onto the ship, there was nothing in the articles stating they were obligated to fight for the king.

The crisis, in spite of the need for hard rowing that resulted in considerable noise, had passed without alarming the guards on shore. Almost as soon as the attack by Drake's men began, the town was aroused. The early morning invasion was of little surprise for the inhabitants had been on nervous alert and expecting an attack from the Cimarrones in the forest.

With Drake's men divided into two parties that were making as much noise and confusion as possible to create the illusion of a large force, the town panicked. The Spanish soldiers were not cowards and many stood their ground fighting hard, but the strategy of the English attacking in two groups convinced the Iberian soldiers that they were being assaulted by overwhelming odds. The Spanish retreated.

The English took possession of the town plaza. From there, a group was sent to the Governor's mansion where they discovered a stack of forty-pound silver bars measuring seventy feet long, twenty feet wide, and twelve feet high. The enormous mass of wealth contained approximately three hundred sixty tons of precious metal, which had been gathered from the mines of both North and South America.

Silver, relative to its value, was too heavy for the raider's captain. It was gold and jewels he sent the men after. The treasure they were after was stored in the king's treasure house, down near the waterfront.

Unknown to his crew, Drake had been struck in the leg by a ball from a well-aimed Spanish arquebus. Bleeding profusely during the foray, Drake had lost so much blood that weakness overtook him and he passed out. One of the attacking sailors, who apparently had liberated some Spanish rum, was quick to give his captain a stiff shot of the fiery booze while others bound up the wounded limb with a scarf. Momentarily the mariner revived, but then again fainted.

Again, the seesaw of fickle luck reversed itself for the treasure-seekers. A torrential tropical rain loosed itself from the skies, wetting much of the powder and in turn, rendering the muskets useless. Also, the same deluge soaked the strings on the longbows. From tense elastic sinews, the bowstrings became slack pieces of gut with no power to catapult an arrow.

Meanwhile, those sent to the waterfront treasure house were having their own troubles. The stout depository walls were not yielding to the efforts of the men trying to open a way to the gold and jewels. Also, another threat to the enterprise manifested. The Spanish soldiers had by then discovered the small size of the raiding force and were regrouping and attacking.

Necessity demanded retreat for the English. There would be another day to fight again the hated Spanish. Gathering up their captain and other wounded, of which there were many, the British crews fought their way back to the beach and their boats.

Perhaps the sailor with the captured rum poured it all into Captain Drake, or maybe it just went the way of any fine stimulant that finds itself in a group of seamen, but in any event, the crew was apparently without a courage bracer as they pulled away from shore, and they resolved not to leave the area empty-handed.

The Spanish wine ship, which had arrived in the harbor only a few hours earlier, was boarded. Her crew was presented with many sharp edged invitations to present themselves ashore, which they complied with posthaste. The wine ship was now proclaimed English, and Drake's men removed themselves and their new vessel to the Isle of Bastimentos, which was just outside the mouth of the bay of Nombre de Dios.

English and Spanish accounts of the raid are naturally

biased in favor of the nation producing a particular account. English records would like to infer the wounding of Francis Drake was the cause for abandonment of the project. Spanish works say that the valorous Spanish soldiers drove off the weak-hearted Britons. In reality, it was most probably the tropical downpour of rain and stout treasure house walls that eventually furnished the turning point from English aggression to retreat.

Drake's force was small. He had necessarily relied on surprise and swiftness of execution to produce a successful raid. By necessity, his men were bound to work in the open, while Spanish defenders were able to snipe from inside buildings, thus it was Drake's powder charges that suffered most from the sky's deluge. In all probability, the walls of the treasure house might have been breached if only a little more time could have been spent in the endeavor. But with their firepower greatly diminished, those attempting to break into the vault could not be defended by the others. Prudence would dictate a hasty withdrawal. Thus, the outcome of the raid on Nombre de Dios could have been one of a different nature, had not the weather favored the Spanish.

GOLDEN HINDE

CHAPTER 8

BASTIMENTOS WAS AN excellent resting place for the defeated English. As the name implies, there was food here for the men as they stopped to bind up their wounds and rest from their exertions. Undoubtedly, the Canary wine that had so recently been carried in the Spanish ship traveled well with the chickens and garden products of the island. The men of Britain were safe here. With the appropriate wine vessel as an escape vehicle, even the possible arrival of a Spanish gunboat posed little problem.

Drake's army rested two days on the tiny tract of land surrounded by water. While there, a Spanish officer came ashore under a flag of truce. It is this event that defines the Devonshire sailor's men as a disciplined force rather than a motley gang of undependable marauders. If they had been the latter, chances are the Iberian officer would never have reached shore. The gritty soldier could easily have been used for target practice when only a few yards offshore.

No doubt the Spanish officer wanted to reconnoiter Drake's camp to see how many men the raider had with him, information when carried back to the mainland would define the defense preparations in case of another attack on the town. The truce flag necessitated the services of a brave man, a performance that certainly did not go unnoticed by Francis Drake who was known as a fair man. Throughout his life he would treat such brave men, regardless of nationality, with honor and respect.

The truce messenger said he wished to discover if the attacker of Nombre de Dios was Drake, as he had heard, and if the arrows used in the raid were poisoned. The man was informed that indeed, he was dealing with Francis Drake. Also, Drake informed him, "I do not use poisoned arrows when fighting any enemy." The wounded Spanish soldiers were safe to have their arrow injuries treated the same as any other wound.

With typical Drake courtesy, an invitation to dine was extended to the Spaniard. Courtesy should not be confused with a dilution of strength of purpose, however. While dining on the best the Englishman had to offer, including some fine, recently liberated Canary wine, the courteous officer from the mainland was informed that he should convey to the Governor of Nombre de Dios that said gentleman could well hold open his eyes and watch closely the treasure that was sent back to Spain, for Drake, if God would grant him life and liberty to do so, would appropriate some of the rich harvest the Iberians took from the earth.

The losses acquired at Rio de la Hacha, San Juan de Ulloa, and now at Nombre de Dios, plus the commercial hardships that rich Spain inflicted on England by means of the abundant New World treasures, made Drake a grimly determined man. Only a man with supreme personal discipline could treat an enemy officer with courtesy under such conditions.

Two days had passed since the arrival of the battle-worn privateers on the island of Bastimentos and little was to be gained by remaining any longer. Island stores were taken aboard the captured wine ship, the small boats painters were fastened astern, and sail was set for the Isles of Pines where James Ranse and the rest of the crews were guarding the ships.

Scarcely had Drake retreated from the treasure city and headed to the island, that his nimble mind was working on another plan to obtain an English share of the riches of the western hemisphere.

One of the principal Spanish commercial routes across the Isthmus of Panama used a water passage up the Chagres

River from the gulf coast towards the Pacific and the town of Venta Cruz. From there, the remaining five leagues to Panama on the Pacific side were traversed by mule train.

European-produced goods destined for the west coasts of both continents and the East Indies were unloaded from the galleons of Spain onto small frigates at the mouth of the Chagres. These small boats, of up to sixteen tons burden, thence sailed, poled, and were pulled up the Chagres to Venta Cruz. There, at the small village, cargo would be unloaded and placed upon the backs of mules in loads weighing up to three hundred pounds per animal. The mule trains slowly wound their way along the twisting jungle trail towards the sea on the west. Many times, traveling single file, these mule trains would string out for several miles.

On the western side of the isthmus, the mules would be loaded with silver, gold and other products from the shores of the Mar del Sur, or Sea of the South, as the Spanish had named the Pacific Ocean. If a Manila galleon arrived at Acapulco, the terminal point of her long voyage from the Moluccas Islands, much of her cargo transshipped on the Lima galleon would be carried to Venta Cruz where it would be unloaded to await the arrival of the Chagres boats from the gulf side.

Undaunted by his recent failure at the treasure shipping terminal of Nombre de Dios, and ready once again to make an effort at laying hold of some Spanish wealth, Drake sent his brother, John Drake, and a crew member, Ellis Hixom, to explore the Chagres and reconnoiter the mule trail.

When the river was too low for loaded boats to travel, mules carried the cargos the entire distance across the isthmus. It was Drake's plan to recruit the help of the Cimarrones in capturing a gold and silver-laden mule train. The Cimarrones, having heard of Drake from the liberated timber cutters on the Isles of Pines, had made it known that they were available to help.

After the revelation of the Nombre de Dios raid results, and the outline of the new project to singe the Spanish beards, James Ranse bowed out of the partnership so recently formed. The recently completed raid had not been a complete failure, as a considerable amount of silver bars from the huge storage pile had been liberated by the retiring English. With his share of this booty and with what he had acquired before falling in with Drake and his men, Ranse was willing to leave well enough alone. He felt as though the Spanish had been stirred up enough and feared that the whole of the Caribbean gulf would become a virtual hornet's nest of armed Iberians searching for the privateers. So, Ranse set his sails for home and England.

In all likelihood Francis Drake was relieved to have the alliance disconnected. There was still much that could be accomplished by bold men. This was not the time to include over-cautious men as part of the group. Before the sails from Ranse's ships had disappeared from view, Drake's crew was preparing their ships for a new venture to furnish more financial lining for their silver-hungry pockets.

Drake reasoned that perhaps news of his raid had not yet reached the Spanish city of Cartagena because Nombre de Dios was a considerable distance from the other city. By land, the road through the jungle between the two towns was a long and difficult one. No Spanish sails had been seen, so perhaps Ranse was wrong and Drake's presence was not known to all of the gulf ports. Cartagena, the capitol of the Spanish Main, would be their next port of call. Once again, the plan was for a swift bold stroke at whatever treasure was available.

It would appear as though Francis Drake was, at that time, nothing more than a pirate and raider against Spain. However, this is just an illusion created by documents put forth for "official" records of both Spain and England. The prize of the new world, with the dominance of Spain over this land, had created a conflict embracing all the concepts of war except open declared conflict between the two nations. Spanish records label Drake as a pirate sanctioned by Elizabeth I. This enabled the peninsula crown to demand redress from England for the depredations instigated by the redheaded corsair. England, on the other hand, officially rejected any official connection with Drake, disclaiming any knowledge of his seafaring actions, also piously promising to chastise him if British officials should find him guilty of such "distasteful actions."

The truth, of course, was that Francis Drake was an agent of money-poor England. His task to spy on Spanish operations in the Caribbean and along the coastlines needed to be financed by dipping into the Spanish treasures whenever possible. There is little doubt that Elizabeth had considerable share in Drake's ventures. Spain knew this, and England was well aware of the Spanish knowledge. It was simply a war without declaration, in which any action was sanctioned and then immediately denied and apologized for by both parties. In later centuries, such a situation would be labeled a "cold war." This deadly game between England and Spain, sometimes flaring into open war, was to continue until the nineteenth century when the North American continent was finally divided between the United States, England, and Mexico.

Drake's raid, soon to be executed against Cartagena, on the surface appears to be a foolish move of a fly attacking a beehive, but underneath, the true reason undoubtedly involves coastal reconnaissance and harbor mapping of the enemy territory. Such vital information was need by England. With a prize so large as the New World, any and all information concerning the land was valuable to the extreme. Spain was certainly not unaware of the real cause for Drake and other British navigators to be on the gulf coasts.

The Spanish government maintained a strict control of all written material leaving the Americas for Europe. Not only the largest and most seaworthy of the galleons carried official dispatches. The men entrusted as couriers were instructed to destroy all state papers in the event of the possibility of their falling into enemy hands. Thus, if the English were to gain true information about the western hemisphere, it must be by first-hand examination and by the experience of dedicated Englishmen.

According to the ancient records available concerning the Cartagena raid, Drake now had five vessels under his command with which he made a landfall at the islands of Barncardo, approximately fifty-five miles from the harbor entrance of the capitol city. At Cartagena, as had been with

Nombre de Dios, the scheme was to enter the harbor with small boats. The islands were the closest place where the large ships could be left with any degree of safety. Spanish galleons traveling between Cartagena and Nombre de Dios would be well to the north of this haven. Small enemy pinnaces, or dispatch boats, which coasted from headland to headland, would be inside or to the east of the islands by at least ten miles, a distance from which a man in a small boat would not be able to detect the English ships.

Again, using the tactics proven to be so successful, the small boats slipped toward their objective under cover of the tropical darkness. Barely within the jaws of the harbor, the silently rowing men suddenly came upon a small frigate quietly swinging on her anchor in the glass-smooth water. Carefully muffled movements of the British sailors as they boarded the ship proved to be unnecessary, for when they gained the frigate's deck, they were greeted by the only crewman aboard, an elderly seaman who was "standing anchor watch." The old sailor informed them that the rest of the crew had gone ashore to "fight over a woman."

Having no grandiose thoughts of standing off Drake and his men single-handedly, the Spaniard readily answered questions put to him concerning ships in the harbor, sailors in the town, and future plans. He also informed them that only an hour earlier, a dispatch boat had arrived bringing news of the presence of Francis Drake and his Nombre de Dios raid. Apparently Drake's flotilla of shallow draft boats and the Spanish message-carrying vessel had almost traveled abreast for the fifty miles from the Bernardo islands.

Here it is appropriate to hypothesize Drake's actions and intents as they probably occurred, rather than as they have been recorded by either English or Spanish writings. England's records are no more reliable than Spain's regarding accuracy because of her efforts to conceal information from the enemy.

It can be logically surmised that one of Drake's smaller boats was investigating the harbor of Cartagena, while the crews in the other pull boats were not only attempting to convince the Spanish that they should dispose of some of their wealth in order to finance the evening's efforts, but were also creating a diversion to claim the attention of the Iberians and lure them away from the areas of planned activity in the harbor.

Contrary to general thought, even in the darkest of nights, if it is not raining or foggy, there is sufficient visibility for experienced boatmen to find their way about in a harbor. One of the pinnaces, or more probably a small jolly boat with only three men, could measure the width of the harbor entrance and record the channel depth and location simply by the man at the oars counting his strokes as he pulled across from point to point at the jaws. The leadsman, when retrieving the line after each cast, would count the fathom market knots as they passed through his hands. The third man in the boat would be scratching figures or marks on a soft lead plate with a sharp, pointed stylus. A great deal of sounding information could be obtained in the darkness, then in the early dawn and at first light, through a few minutes sketching by a competent artist who could place ship anchorages, dock locations and possibly even buoys, thus completing a useable charting of the enemy harbor.

The old man on watch aboard the Spanish frigate had informed Francis and his crew that there was a galleon anchored closer to the land inside the harbor. This ship had only recently arrived from Seville. Its cargo had already been adjusted for the port, some taken off and more put aboard. The vessel was due to sail for San Domingo in the morning.

Silently, the assaulting pinnaces headed for the ship of Seville. The cargo carrier was a vessel of two hundred and fifty tons displacement. Drake and his men had been spotted by the deckwatch who hailed them in the darkness. Apparently the galleon crew had been alerted to the recent conflict at Nombre de Dios. While the shouted Spanish challenge still rang in the air, the English corsairs, with no urging from their leader, strained at the oars, surging their boats hard ahead to bring them up against the side of the intended prize. The high sides of the plate ship proved difficult to scale, and the deck was not conquered without the noisy confusion of shots, clashing arms and shouting men. In short order, however, the resistance of the Iberians was overcome with their fate being "battened under hatches." Most of the defeated crew had already been below decks, getting in some bunk time before sailing call in the morning. It can be speculated that the "fight" recorded in the records may even have been one of Drake's own making, for he was a master in the art of diversion. Stealing a well-armed vessel with a sleeping crew and then making a large amount of noise at the proper time would most effectively conceal the actions of another segment of the assault crew, while at the same time commanding the attention of a nervous town population. Also, it would be a relatively safe operation.

Command attention it did. Church bells large and small began tolling, cannon started booming, and a force of both mounted and foot troops raced down the shoreline parallel to the ship. There was nothing the landsmen could do. Neither the cannoneers, nor the troops dare fire on the vessel because they really did not know what was taking place aboard the Seville galleon. Cannon shot could destroy a vessel still under the charge of their own people, or having been re-taken by them. Or an arquebus ball, a lucky shot at that distance, might kill Spanish and not English. So, as the bells tolled out their defiance and fear, the cannons fired at open spaces of water, and the troops waved their arms menacingly, Francis Drake calmly upped anchor and sailed out of Cartagena with one of King Philip's treasure galleons, taking her to the shelter of the Isla de Tierra Bomba, just outside the harbor.

The following morning two more small hulls were captured outside the harbor and, with typical Drake good humor and civility—attributes fully admitted by his enemy, the crews of the little frigates were set ashore.

Aboard the two boats had been couriers with official letters of advice to the Cartagena officials. The missives contained instructions on how to deal with Drake should he show up in those parts. The dispatch carriers were allowed to retain their messages, along with the red-haired Englishmen's good wishes!

CHAPTER 9

IN MANY OF the "adjusted" official documents put forth by the two jousting nations of Spain and England, there were lengthy weird passages of incomprehensible explanation concerning events taking place on both land and sea. These unintelligible record segments are products of government scribes endeavoring to create diversion and confusion on paper for those of the enemy who would carefully inspect the published document for scraps of useful information. One of these outlandish and laughable explanations appears in records of Francis Drake at this point in his daring career.

According to the annals, Francis Drake wanted to create another ruse to distract the Spanish, possibly hoping to have them believe he had left the Darian coast and was headed for home. So, he burned and swamped the little *Swan*, to leave it derelict and drifting in the sailing rack between Cartagena and Nombre de Dios.

This exploit may have been staged to appear as though the group had met with a Spanish gunboat and been defeated, thus cutting pursuit from those who were by now looking for Drake with a vengeance. As communication between ship and shore was nonexistent in those days, it would be a considerable time before the Spanish were able to determine that none of their vessels had engaged in a battle with Drake and his men.

According to the Crown's statement, the *Swan* and her crew were the pride and joy of Drake's brother John, so

Francis Drake had Thomas Moone, a carpenter, sneak into the bilge at night with a "spike gimlet" with which he bored three holes near the ship's keel. The next morning, Drake took his brother fishing. After the fishing trip and their arrival back at the *Swan*, Drake purportedly asked his brother, "Why is your ship so low in the water?"

The foregoing piece of record is so utterly ridiculous that it hardly warrants attention, except that to many shore-side dwellers it may appear plausible. Still, anyone who has spent time around the brine and on small boats cannot stand idly by without making some comment on this bit of nonsense.

There are several reasons for disbelief about the passage. First, it only takes a small amount of water in the hull, acquired during the night, for a fo'casle crewmember to notice. Secondly, pump duty is carried out periodically. This is a chore that is not relished by any seaman and the man at the end of the handle can soon tell if the last sailor "pumped her clean" or was derelict in his work. Wooden vessels all leak to a certain extent, and after a few days at sea, the crew can tell to the quart, and number of pump handle strokes, how much time will have to be spent at each pumping. Any change in the amount of bilge water would be noticed and investigated at once. The tale that Drake took his brother fishing and returned to find the *Swan* deep in the water is ridiculous.

Drake had additional business on the Darian coast. Supposedly his plan was to capture more Peruvian gold, but in actuality the foremost reason was probably to reconnoiter more of Spain's holdings and explore the land, its rivers and harbors.

Drake wanted to learn a great deal more about the Isthmus of Panama. True, much information had been obtained by the English crown from sailors and spies, but the day of the double espionage agent had dawned many centuries before, which meant all knowledge of the Americas must be double-checked by the first-hand exploration of known trustworthy agents of the crown.

The voyage had thus far been a profitable one in spite of the reverses at Nombre de Dios. Apparently, some of the crews wished to let well enough alone, not push their luck any further, and return home. The crew would share well in the booty thus far obtained and probably rightly reasoned that by now the Spanish would be mad as hornets. A goodly share of the men in Drake's ships had little wish to remain in the area.

A grumbling crew in such a situation is not a new occurrence, especially if they envision being able to afford large quantities of ale and numerous pretty girls when they step ashore at home port. The scuttling of the *Swan* and revelation of a new and more daring venture must have brought forth loud protests and lengthy orations in the fo'castles and other places the sailors went, beyond the hearing of Captain Drake. It is doubtful if any dared cross the wide forbidden void of communication between crew and captain, for this was a no-man's land needfully respected by both factions.

Low key grumbling, growling, and protesting is a sailor's prerogative, but even the loudest of the protestors knew that when he first placed a foot on the deck back in England, he had freely chosen to go aboard because of his faith in the soundness of the vessels and his faith in the leadership of Francis Drake.

Once the *Swan* was scuttled and burned and a new strike underway, the die was cast with no turning point. The grousing of the crew diminished and their enthusiasm for the new venture replaced their wish to return to England. The captain's plan was to attack the Spanish mule trains bringing gold and silver to Nombre de Dios from Panama. They might all get rich!

With the command ship *Pasha*, the two hundred fifty-ton captured Spanish galleon, and the pinnaces, the English force set out to establish a base camp in a secluded port where both vessels and men could be well hidden. The rest of the captured vessels were scuttled and burned, perhaps along with the *Swan*. Records indicate that in all probability, the anchorage chosen was in today's Golfo de San Blas, at a place then called Cathwas Bay. The site was near the current town of Mandinga.

At that out-of-the-way place, where detection by Spanish vessels was deemed to be at a minimum, huts were built, forges set up, and all things done to prepare for a long stay of several months. It was by then the rainy season when much of the land was a soggy, muddy area of swamp and near-swamp. At that time of year, the mule trains carrying Pacific shores treasure across the Isthmus were not in motion due to the difficulties of travel. Silver plate and gold bars would have been stored in Panama until travel conditions improved.

To feed Drake's force of men, large quantities of food were required. A considerable amount of stores had been obtained from the captured prizes, but this was by no means sufficient to sustain the group during the four or five-month wait before the expedition against the treasure train could be executed.

Leaving Fort Diego, as the encampment came to be called in honor of the Negro who had deserted the Spanish at Nombre de Dios to travel with the English, Drake set out with two of the pinnaces and part of the men to "trade" with the Spanish for victuals and any other stores that would be needed at the base camp.

Brother John Drake was left in command of the fort, and, as Diego suggested, he was instructed to go into the jungle to try to make contact with the Cimarrones. The purpose of this penetration would be to endeavor to secure the Cimarrones' help in attacking the treasure-laden mule train when it set out across the narrow neck of land between the Atlantic and Pacific oceans. John Drake's other chore was to proceed to the wreck of a caravel that had cast upon a nearby beach, and remove from it the hull planking to be used for construction of additional fortifications and houses.

The record is vague concerning this caravel wreck, but there is a possibility that it was the *Perivil of Hull*, one of John Garrett's ships. Garrett, remember, was the man who left the lead plate warning at Port Pheasant.

Clearly, Drake had the need by then to create another false impression upon the minds of the Spanish if he were to keep secret the whereabouts of his base of operations. The deception fabricated with the scuttling of the *Swan* and the captured prizes may have lured the Iberian officials into believing the "Devil Drake" had set sail for home or perished on the *Swan*. Nevertheless, they would be quick to organize their forces once it was discovered that Drake had tricked them and remained in the area.

To have returned close to Nombre de Dios would certainly be a move the Spanish would hardly expect. Drake's camp was within fifty miles of the treasure port, the placing of which was a bold maneuver that had to be protected. They had to create the implication that the Britishers had remained close to Cartagena; possibly establishing themselves somewhat south of that capitol city. Thus, in the search for added stores, it would be imperative not to take any vessels west of Cartagena. In fact, it would be just as vital not to be seen in that area at all. That precaution, hopefully, would keep any search for the corsair at least two hundred miles away from Fort Diego.

Again, it can be conjectured that provision-hunting was not the sole reason for the foray with the pinnaces. There was always more coastline to inspect, sound, and chart.

The Magdalena River entrance was the first "port of call" for the pinnaces. This important harbor where the export city of Barranquilla, Columbia is now located, was a supply district for the victualling yards at Cartagena. The Magdalena is one of the longest rivers in South America, its origin more than seven hundred miles way, within one hundred miles of the Pacific Ocean. It was at this river that Drake obtained two frigates as prizes, loaded them with beef he bought from the Indians, and with biscuit, preserves and other foodstuffs obtained under protest from the Spanish storehouses and coasting frigates.

It was a fast shopping trip. Within ten days, Francis Drake returned to Fort Diego with the needed food, plus in all probability important additional charting observations for the mariners of England. Meanwhile, during his absence, under the direction of his brother John Drake, the fort position had been changed to a new and more advantageous location a few miles distant from the original site. Other precautions had been undertaken to assure success of the venture. In several places there had been cached depots of food, guns, and other stores in case they would be needed in haste at some later date. Too, they might serve well someone on a later voyage to the Indies.

The next roadstead called upon was Tolu in the Golfo de Morrosquillo, sixty miles south of Cartagena. It has been said that here Drake robbed orchards and fruit gardens. Perhaps this is true, but in face of having recently procured many preserves, some of which must have been fruit, to go orchard robbing as a prime move seems to leave room for question. Maybe, while some of the crew were "stealing apples," others were adding Tolu as just another anchorage and port to measure, diagram and paint for the good of Elizabeth and the crown.

Further north towards Cartagena, the daring Englishman and his men, in the little pinnaces, again entered the harbor where several small prizes were taken. Bad weather forced the raiders to seek refuge inside the harbor where Spanish troops continually harassed them in an effort to drive them back out to sea and into the storm.

Forced to lay away from the shore in the small, open boats continually buffeted by the choppy harbor waters, high wind and rain, Drake and his crew were extremely uncomfortable in their cramped quarters. To add to their plight, their food was running low.

The Spanish shot off their arquebus, but were unable to reach the small English boats, so they attempted an attack with a ship's boat and a large canoe. The Britishers beat off the assault and in retaliation, the bold Drake attempted an attack of his own. This "sea battle" ebbed almost as abruptly as it began. Prudence overcame valor once again and the Iberians retreated. Pulling frantically at their oars, the Spaniards beat a hasty return to shore-side defenses, where they took up pot-shotting at the English intruders. Only when the coming of evening took away the shooting light did they give up their efforts.

The next day the weather calmed somewhat when the rains stopped, but the wind continued to be hard westerly and thus there was no possibility of Drake and his men beating against it for a return to the fort and base camp. Cartagena was, by then, only too aware of their presence, so the only way out for the provision hunters was to go back to the Rio Magdalena.

The Spanish were obviously well alerted to the presence of their enemies. The port of Magdalena proved to be on the alert. Warehouses along the river were deserted and livestock had been driven into the hills, out of the Englishmen's reach.

Again Drake and his crew pushed northward, setting their sails for Santa Marta, and once again they were discovered by the Spanish and forced to leave. Nothing is stated about this landing in the old chronicles, for certainly it would not be put forth for public consumption that Drake was in the area. But again the reader would be safe to assume that again, Francis Drake and his bold-as-brass crew had probably surveyed and charted one more Spanish harbor.

At Santa Marta the gloomy weather once more picked up to create a lumpy, bone-jarring sea for the men in the open boats. The long period without exercise ashore and the lack of good food was beginning to make sullen even the most genial members of the expedition. The pinnaces were continually taking slops and spray over the side and the men had not been in dry clothes for several days. Undoubtedly by then the chafing of their garments against continually wet skin had created saltwater boils, a most miserable and painful affliction. They were as near to mutiny as a faithful crew can get.

Drake wanted to push on yet another one hundred miles eastward to the mouth of the Rio de la Hacha, possibly to reconnoiter one more harbor, but his crew was beginning to balk. They protested about the lack of food to get them that far. Captain Drake was adamant. "We can make it," he said. Conceivably, the crew of rough men, both tired and pious, offered a prayer and asked His guidance. Drake pointed the bowstem of his pinnace to the north, and the other boat, with its grumbling but faithful crew, followed.

Perhaps it was luck or faith, or possibly a little of both, which brought sight of a sail to one of the tiny vessels when it topped the crest of a wave. At last, a chance for a prize and some food!

The sea had once more partially moderated, so the chase was on! The prospects of good food and wine, plus the chance to walk a deck instead of being confined to a tortuous, skin-scoring board seat, eliminated the pain of cramped legs, numbed hands, and the stabbing pains of the saltwater boils.

If they could catch the Spanish vessel she would be theirs, for the unsuspecting ship was captained by a peaceful merchantman and no match for the well-armed English. It took two hours to close the gap between the vessels and get near enough for the English to fire menacing shots. Only a few rounds over their heads were necessary to convince the Spanish sailors that resisting would bring on a shorter life.

The prize this time was a ship of approximately ninety tons displacement, a fair-sized vessel and certainly worthy of keeping. In her hold was a generous supply of food and other cargo, all of which could be put to good use by the expedition. The now-prisoner Spanish seamen were set ashore and Drake and his crew ate heartily then set sail for Fort Diego.

GOLDEN HINDE

CHAPTER 10

THE FIRST REPORT the daring seaman received upon entering the harbor was of the death of his brother, John. Francis Drake had relied heavily on John for the success of the venture and they were deeply attached. Contrary to Francis' orders when left with the pinnaces, John and a few other members of the remaining crew had endeavored to capture a small Spanish vessel. That was a bold, reckless act that ended with John Drake being split by a Spanish pikeman.

The vessel attacked by John Drake had been loaded with Iberian soldiers, evidently prowling the sea in an attempt to capture the Englishman. Other news revealed that the Spanish had discovered and rifled some of the English magazines along the coast where captured gold and extra equipment had been stashed. In response, Francis Drake decided to remain under cover and not attempt any more prize taking. Chancing capture, or even a hard fight, would not be beneficial to the operation at that time.

Four weeks of inactivity advanced the season to where the weather was noticeably changing from winter into summer. The downside was that the men were beginning to chafe with restlessness and it was then that another disaster struck the expedition.

Ten crewmen were seized with fever and sickness and most of them died within a few days after becoming afflicted. Soon others became ill. Thirty were sick at the same time.

Drake, who had the reputation of being a good doctor, assisted the project's surgeon and together they worked almost day and night to save the men. Indeed, the surgeon himself became ill, recovered, and again tended the sick. Then came the cruelest blow of all, Joseph, another of Drake's brothers, passed away. It would be understandable if, at that point, Drake decided to give up the expedition's goals and head his ships for home. But this Englishman was one who never listened to any inner voice crying out "Quit!" Instead, Drake ordered an autopsy preformed on his brother's body so that information about the sickness might be obtained so others could benefit.

Even the ship's surgeon never gave up, for he concocted a potion of drugs he believed might be of help and, not wishing to endanger any of the men, tried the experimental medicine on himself but died as a result. By then, thirty-two crewmen died as a result of sickness, combat or other causes. Beyond question, many of those remaining expressed satisfaction with the booty already in hand and indicated their desire to return home. Their captain, however, was of more resolute determination. Francis Drake had voyaged to examine the lands and harbors of the new world and to relieve Spain's King Philip of his treasure. His job was not yet finished. No one would go home.

Past friendships with the Cimarrones had stood well for the party. When the English were sick, the ex-slaves brought them food. Now they came forth with the news of a Spanish fleet gathering at Nombre de Dios. The tidings created a burst of activity in the camp for all knew the treasure-laden mule train would soon be leaving the Pacific port of Panama, headed toward Nombre de Dios.

Thirty Cimarrones offered their services as guides and fighting men ready to attack the treasure trains. Many of Drake's men were still infirm, resulting in only eighteen able-bodied seamen prepared to set forth on the island trek. On Shrove Tuesday, February 3, the column of forty-eight corsairs plunged forth into the dense jungle to intercept the bell-ornamented mules of the Spanish columns.

Good, silver, and other valuable commodities obtained

from Spanish colonies on the Pacific Coast of the Americas were funneled through the Port of Panama, thence across the isthmus and on to Spain. The rich mines of Peru, New Galicia, Sonora, Sinaloa, and the Californias all contributed to the tons of silver bars stacked annually in the streets of Panama. From there the bounty would be carried over land by long strings of pack mules interspersed with their Indian drivers. The line of mules sometimes stretched over a mile. Then, as today, the Isthmus of Panama offered the shortest and fastest route between oceans.

The isthmus is approximately forty miles across from the Port of Panama on the Pacific side, to today's Port of Colon on the Atlantic coast. Before the building of the Panama Canal, it was possible to traverse much of the narrow strip of land with small boats by way of the Chagres River. The Spanish used this Rio Chagres to good advantage. Timing of the crossing was of major importance, for the Chagres needed to be at high level from heavy rains, and yet the jungle trails must be dry enough to withstand the continuous cutting action of many copper mule shoes, otherwise they would transform the trail into a bog. Only when the trails were driest could transport across the breadth of the isthmus be done entirely by mule.

With the Changres running full enough for boat level, the mule trail necessary when Drake arrived was only about fifteen miles long. The trail connected Panama to Venta Cruces, a small village on the waterway at the head of navigation near today's city of Gamboa.

Shallow draft vessels of approximately seventeen tons displacement were used by the Iberians to ascend the Rio Chagres to Venta Cruces and, once there, to await the treasure-laden mule trains. Francis Drake intended to intercept the animal transport columns before they reached the river transshipping point.

In keeping with other probes of the expedition, the surveillance of Panama harbor was undoubtedly of highest importance to the distinguished mariner of the Tudor queen's service. Francis Drake was the first Englishman to view the all-important Iberian Pacific harbor with the express purpose of observing. Drake not only had the trained eye of a sea captain whose goal was to con a vessel into the haven, he was also a naval man noticing both natural and man-made defenses.

Hacking and pushing their way through sometimes almost impenetrable jungle growth, Drake and his men ascended a spur of the Cordillera de San Blas. It was a strenuous job for the Englishmen because they carried both weapons and machetes. The friendly black Cimarrones had the most difficult role, for they had volunteered to carry all the supplies for the raiding group. The willingness of the black rebels to assist Drake could be doubted by some readers, for the English were engaged in slavery and few treated the captives well. But Francis Drake, even though he had engaged in the slave trade, had a reputation of behaving with civility to the Africans and all other men. Even his enemies, including the Spanish, lauded the man for his fair treatment and compassion when dealing with prisoners.

Led by Chief Pedro of the Cimarrones, the column of sailors and allies climbed slowly up the ridge between San Blas Bay and Puerto Escribanas. Pedro had promised Drake that when they reached the highest point of the mountain ridge that lay athwart the isthmus, the adventurous mariner would be able to see the great Pacific. In fact, both seas, the Atlantic and the Pacific, could be viewed from the same high vantage point.

Four days of slow, strenuous ascension through beautiful forest and sometimes dense jungle brought the small force to the top of the mountain chain. At that crest, the Cimarrones had a clearing and several huts and the tallest tree had been shorn of all view-interfering foliage. Near the tree's crown a small observation platform had been constructed. The mountaintop elevation was nearly two thousand feet. Twenty-five miles to the south, they could see the Gulf of Panama and the Pacific Ocean. Back to the north fifteen miles was the Caribbean Sea and the Atlantic Ocean. To the northeast, thirteen miles away, the men could look down on the Gulf of San Blas, the place of their departure. It was at this location that Francis Drake, in the flowery language of his time, vowed to John Oxenham (sometimes spelled Oxnam), a lieutenant of his company, that someday he would sail the Pacific and be the first Englishman to sail the sea of the Spanish. The equally bold Oxenham replied that if the captain did not remove him from his company, then by God's grace he would follow Drake.

Unbeknown to the two friends, John Oxenham would be the first Tudor subject to ply the waters of the "Spanish Lake." The furious Spanish, at a later time, would enact a grim toll for Oxenham's intrusion by hanging this rash Englishman in Lima, Peru. And at an even later time, Drake would make the Spanish pay dearly for this act.

It was probably near this crest of land, where the two Englishmen were talking, that the Spanish explorer Vasco Nunez de Balboa first saw the Pacific Ocean in 1513. He, like Drake and Oxenham, had also vowed to sail that beautiful water. In fact, no sailor could gaze upon such a sight without making that solemn promise to himself.

A short rest for the company gave each member a turn to climb the tree's observation post with its hewn notches and limb stubs for steps, and set their eyes upon the two seas. They paused briefly for a repast, their stomachs always hungry due to the strenuous exertion of climbing, and then headed westward for the downhill trek toward the Pacific.

Two more days of traveling through jungle and forest brought a change of terrain. In front of the group stretched an open plain with low rolling hillocks covered with Pampas grass. At that point a new threat revealed itself.

It would not do to be accidentally discovered by a wandering Spaniard while the column of men was out in the open. The forest and jungle had furnished good protection from discovery, but an open plain could reveal all. Cimarrone scouts were sent ahead to search the countryside for the enemy while the remaining group of men endeavored to conceal themselves by crossing the open ground in the small swales and gullies between the hummocks. For another two days they moved carefully and cautiously across the plain. Occasionally, as they stopped for rest, some of the men would guardedly crawl to the top of a nearby rise to observe the ground ahead. Many times, glimpses of the Gulf of Panama could be seen.

The third day of the open savanna crossing, February 14, brought the corsairs close to the outskirts of Panama City and alongside the mule road to Venta Cruces. Here the danger of discovery became most acute, for at any time a roving Spaniard, or a converted Indian, might stumble onto the expedition. Even though all the men were subject to extreme caution, tension hung heavy in the atmosphere. The accidental noise of a forty-eight-man group could unexpectedly occur simultaneously, creating a relatively loud sound and thus warning the enemy.

Drake dispersed his men into units of two and three to crawl through the high grass along a waterless riverbed to a small group of trees. Once there, they would be comparatively free from detection but could easily observe the town. Pedro, the Cimarrone leader, sent one of his men into the treasure city to scout the activity of the habitation in relation to the forthcoming departure of the treasure from the mules. The spy's dress, appearance, and knowledge of the Spanish would allow him to enter the gates of the city and wander about the town unchallenged.

If the mule trains were being readied, the Cimarrones would be able to estimate the number of animals and the burdens of the first line destined to string out toward Venta Cruces.

Francis Drake offered a short prayer for the success of the black man and the eventual raid upon the mule train. But there was other work to be done and no time to tarry; God would have to be trusted more and prayed to less. The intrepid mariner set off by himself to a vantage point above Panama City and the harbor where all of the road and town could be seen. He sited himself in a location that would furnish the best naval information to his queen and other superiors.

Again we must conclude that this versatile seaman calmly used his well-known artistic abilities to sketch the harbor of Panama with its defenses, docks, roadsteads and channels. This time there would be no small boats with which to carry a leadsman about the harbor in the dark of night. Instead, harbor distances would have to be estimated from a single vantage point. Channel locations would be placed in proportion and their depths estimated by observation of the sizes of the vessels plying in and out. This duty was one Drake was to carry out at many harbors on later dates when he sailed the Pacific in his own vessel.

When Drake arrived back at the grove of trees where the rest of the party was encamped, Pedro's man had already returned. The Cimarrone spy came back with astounding news several hours before his return arrival was expected. Shortly after entering the port city of Panama, the investigating black had encountered friends who had considerable knowledge of town affairs. They said a large treasure galleon of three hundred tons burden was laying at Nombre de Dios waiting to take on Pacific coast cargo for Spain. They also told the Cimarrone that the grand personage of the Treasurer of Lima desired to travel to Europe on that vessel and that he and his family, with fourteen laden mules, were starting that same evening for the opposite coast. The resident Panamanians further related that two large mule trains of fifty animals each would soon start the trek to Nombre de Dios. Nearly half the animals of these two trains would be carrying food and trade goods. The other half of the pack mules would be heavily burdened with gold, silver, and jewels from the mines of the west coasts of the two continents.

The good news, so quickly obtained, was exhilarating to the adventurers and their leader. Immediately, Francis Drake set about making plans to relieve the mules from their weighty loads. It was deemed most prudent for the band to retrace their steps back along the mule trail until they were only a short distance from Venta Cruces. To attack the train after it arrived had the advantage of the gold and silver being transported for them as far as possible by the Spanish. It was in Venta Cruces that Drake and his men would bear off for the coast across the mountains with the captured spoils. At Venta Cruces, the Spanish treasure road led northwestward down the Chagres River, but Francis and his crew would go to the southeast, across the Cordillera to their gulf-side fort.

The men had sufficient time to travel the several miles of return to Venta Cruces. Due to the oppressing heat, the mule trains traveled by night for the better comfort of both men and animals.

The English corsair, in arranging his ambush, stationed his men along the trail at short intervals and in a line calculated to be the length of the man and animal caravan. Thus, when the first mule would be stopped by the concealed men closest to Venta Cruces at the north end of the train, the last animal in line would be stopped and lined up opposite the men at the southern end of the ambush. All hands were cautioned to lie quietly, making neither sound nor move until the leader should blow his whistle, signifying the last mule had moved abreast of the Panama end of the entrapment. At that signal, the attack was to begin.

Only a short time after the ambuscade was in place, the tinkling of harness bells could be heard coming from the direction of Venta Cruces and Nombre de Dios. It was a mule train of supplies headed for Panama. This was an unexpected event. It was important that these muleteers and their guards did not suspect the presence of anyone other than themselves on the trail, or they would give warning to the approaching Lima treasurer and his train.

Perhaps he had imbibed too strongly in brandy as some are wont to assert, or maybe the continuous torment of the hungry mosquitoes was the cause, or perhaps the anxious need for action drove him to it, but in any event one of Drake's men stood up to get a better look at the approaching Spanish. Immediately, he was pulled back down by other members of the group. To the hidden observers, the actions of the man apparently went unseen by the muleteers, for the train continued on at a steady, unbroken pace. True, one of the Spanish merchants accompanying the train spurred his mount forward, but it did not seem to mean anything because of the continued steady pace of the others.

Only a short while after the passing of the Panama-bound cavalcade, bells were again heard. This time they came from the Pacific side of the isthmus, which indicated the Lima treasurer's mule train was approaching the ambush. When the last mule had passed by his hiding place, Francis Drake blew hard on his whistle. The corsairs charged from their places of concealment and the train was theirs. The mule drivers showed no inclination to fight, so immediately the mule packs were opened. But there was no gold and there was no silver.

The muleteers explained. It turned out the feather-brained mariner Robert Pike, the man who had stood up because he wanted a better look at the Panama-bound provision train, had been seen and the mule train coming from Panama had been warned. Thus, the treasurer from Lima had taken his family and gold and made haste to return back down the trail to Panama. The balance of the procession, those animals and their attendants with the food and trade goods, had been ordered to continue on and spring the trap, if one existed. The head muleteer offered more good news in that soon the entire area would be aroused and on the lookout for the English marauders.

Francis Drake was well known for his oratory proficiency when preaching the gospel. It is extremely doubtful that such was the sermon received by the foolish seaman who had so oafishly scuttled the treasure-raiding enterprise. Robert Pike had caused trouble not only for his associates, but for himself as well. His behavior put him in the unenviable position of never being trusted again by his fellow seamen. Pike had sealed his fate, for his reputation would always precede him amongst the seafaring men in the English ports.

The muleteer was, of course, correct in his statement that Drake's presence on the isthmus road would soon be known to the Spanish authority. There was only one thing left to do, and that was to get back to the coast and the ships. The town of Venta Cruces blocked the way of the most direct return route. Prudent men would have circled the settlement to avoid any contact with possible enemies. Drake's men and their leader were no longer prudent. They were disgusted and mad, and no longer interested in the bypassing of any Spaniard. The act of a simpleton had changed a venture of riches into one of disaster and poverty. They would take the shortest route to the ships and if an Iberian was unlucky enough to stand in the way, then let the fool take his chances. The Spanish muleteers were told to get back down the trail as fast as they could run, while the Englishmen were still in a charitable mood. The mules were mounted by the infuriated sailors who, muttering and growling, headed toward Venta Cruces. The men with no mounts walked alongside.

When they were within a short distance of the Spanish pueblo, a guard detachment was encountered. An order to halt and be recognized was countered with a bellow from the disgruntled Drake. A few well-placed words stated they were English and the Spaniards had better get out of the way! The guards were not so easily frightened. They let go with a volley that killed one man and slightly wounded Drake. The Spanish-hating Cimarrones charged forward after the firing of the one-shot arquebuses. The guards fled, racing into the town as fast as their feet could carry them, yelling out about the presence of the English. The populace of the town panicked.

Venta Cruces was a village on the isthmus endowed with a more favorable climate than most other settlements in the area. Consequently, many Spaniards established residences there for their wives during childbearing years. A considerable number of these ladies were living in the pleasant pueblo when Drake and his men came through pillaging for food and booty. The valorous English leader, living up to his reputation for gallantry, assured them they would be treated courteously by all of his men and they need feel no fear.

For the English, unfortunately, very little plunder was found in Venta Cruces, other than foodstuffs. The Cimarrones however, burdened themselves with large amounts of miscellaneous pillage they thought might be useful some future day.

Little time was allowed the raiders for searching the village, for shooting was heard near the edge of town. Pickets left as a rear guard had engaged a force of mounted Spaniards who, when fired upon, had fallen back to regroup. That party of Iberians was larger and better armed than the soldiers

Drake's men had routed when first arriving. After reassembling, the soldiers immediately organized an attack, but by then the English mariner and his force had melted into the forest and were out of sight.

Under forced march, Francis Drake and his men started a hurried return to the ships. There was little chance of the soldiers trying to chase the invading sailors through the jungle, yet prudence was now more relished than the reckless bravery of the first encounter at the edge of the hamlet just vacated. Their recent experience showed there was nothing to be gained from a confrontation. Nothing except an arquebus ball or a saber slash.

GOLDEN HINDE

CHAPTER 11

THE ALARM WAS now out to all Spaniards on the isthmus within notification distance. Drake is still here! Not only were his ships in the Caribbean, but an expeditionary force was on the mainland! Not only must the harbor towns be on the lookout, but the mule trains were in danger!

The trek over the mountains and back to the sea was a trying one for the raiders. By then, the shoes and clothing of most were worn to shreds. Their dispositions were in the same state of disrepair. Growling and grumbling, with their leader periodically adding his forceful opinions of the whole affair, the disgusted and plunderless force finally arrived back at the shore of the Caribbean Sea where their boats were anchored.

The failure of the mule train raid brought forth many thoughts on what the expedition should do next. Some again wanted to sail for home with the spoils they had so far acquired. Others felt the need for more gold bullion and silver plate. The decision was to remain and try again.

Drake decided to raid at sea, for now it would be foolish to immediately attempt another inland raid with Spanish soldiers diligently patrolling the Venta Cruces area. Sea raids would again have to be the means to gain a fatter purse for everyone. Two pinnaces, the *Minion* and the *Bear*, were readied for seawork. The *Bear*, under the command of John

Oxenham, would sail eastward toward Cartagena with the intent of obtaining more victuals for the expedition, by any means. Drake himself would command the pinnace *Minion* and try to stop vessels going to Nombre de Dios with gold and silver for the treasure galleon's cargo.

The skipper and his crew captured a small frigate heading for the Spanish port. On board this vessel was treasure from the rich mines of Veragua. Also aboard was a Genoese pilot who quickly decided to cooperate with his captors when he learned their identity. This gentleman convinced Drake he should attempt the boarding of a frigate laying at Veragua because it had a million dollars worth of gold aboard. The venture was a failure, however, for when an approach to the vessel was made, alert Spanish lookouts sounded the alarm. The pinnace and her crew were no match for the larger force of better-armed men aboard the frigate.

John Oxenham and his men fared better than those of the *Minion*. Their pinnace had encountered and captured a stores-laden vessel. The ship was a staunch, well-built craft that was of too great a value to either burn or leave behind for further use by the Spanish. So, its crew was set ashore. Then, towing the pinnace, Oxenham and his men sailed the frigate to the English fortifications. In the hold of the captured vessel was a great store of maize. On deck were two dozen fat pigs and more than two hundred chickens. Oxenham, sent for food, had a much more successful trip than Drake, who had set out for gold and silver.

The new ship in the rendezvous was careened for bottom scrubbing, scorching and oiling. After additional work on the rigging, Drake and some of his men embarked in the refurbished ex-Spanish vessel to endeavor once more to capture a treasure-laden ship heading for Nombre de Dios. The captive vessel, now under the Englishman's command, was probably well known in the Spanish waters and this deception might have allowed the corsairs to work their way close to a treasure frigate.

No Spanish were seen, but the rovers fell in with a large French ship in need of water. Captained by a mariner from Harve named Le Testu, the vessel and her crew were also seeking Iberian bullion and plate.

Once again Francis Drake was prevailed upon to enter into a partnership. And, as before, he accepted. There was still reluctance on Drake's part to share an enterprise with another captain, but this time he had even less choice because his crew was much smaller than its original size. Perhaps the liaison would be to the advantage of all, for Le Testu had a large crew of seventy men and a fine ship of eighty tons.

The ill-fated expedition across the isthmus, with its resulting failure to capture a silver and gold-laden mule train, had rankled deep in the thoughts of Francis Drake. The chance of a large payday for all the crew had, by a quirk of fate, brought empty pockets to the entire force. Now, with a stronger body of men composed of French, English and Cimarrone forces, perhaps another foray could fill out the remaining wrinkles in the slackness of the purses.

By then it was apparent at that point that the small Spanish treasure frigates could not navigate the Chagres River from Venta Cruces to Colon Bay due to low water, so all treasure and merchandise to be loaded on the galleons for Spain had to traverse the isthmus to Nombre de Dios entirely by mule-back. Evidently the Cimarrones were keeping Drake well informed of Spanish treasure movements for a plan was formulated to trap the mule caravan when it was almost at the gates of the city. Drake reasoned that the guards of Spain's four-legged walking pocketbooks would relax their vigil against raiders when they were almost at the journey's end. The plan was to set an ambush as close to the edge of the town as possible and still be out of hearing of the residents and soldiers stationed there.

The French crew was allowed almost a week to rest and re-provision their ship from the secret caches of the English. The latter part of their latest voyage had been a trying one and they had run low on food and water. Meanwhile, Drake and Le Testu planned the coming raid against the mule trains.

The attacking force this time was to be composed of fifteen of Drake's men, twenty of Le Testu's crew, and the band of Cimarrones. The French captain was somewhat dubious concerning the loyalty of the fierce Cimarrones, but

Drake assured him the half-black, half-Indian men were loyal allies. Drake, of course, knew by experience about the reliability of the warriors, but Le Testu, having no prior association with the Cimarrones remained somewhat nervous about the dark men's involvement.

The sturdy little captured frigate, so recently taken by John Oxenham, was fitted out as a small gunboat to accompany the raiders and two pinnaces. This vessel was left on the west side of Point San Blas, anchored out of sight behind the Cabecas Rocks. The assaulters then took the two pinnaces around the long finger-shaped headland into San Blas Bay where they entered the mouth of the Rio Francisco and traveled inland as far as the river was navigable. At that spot, a boat guard was left behind to return the pinnaces to the frigate, with orders to meet again at this riverbank location in four days. The orders were explicit. They meant exactly four days, no more and no less. Whether at sea or on land, Francis Drake endeavored to be the perfectionist in all details regarding the execution of any maneuver.

This time the overland trek to the ambush site was not so long or arduous. The first pack train raid was a one-way march of seventy miles, plus the climb over the backbone mountain ridge of the isthmus. This time the trek was only twenty miles along the foothills.

Once more the Cimarrones guided the Europeans through the steaming and trackless jungle. Circling around behind Nombre de Dios, they placed their ambush in a location where they could look down upon the town. As planned, Drake set his trap so close to the outskirts of the seaport that blows from the hammers of ship carpenters could be heard as craftsmen worked in the evening hours rather than in the heat of the day. The treasure galleons were being readied for their voyage across the Atlantic.

There was little worry this time that a crew man with one too many pannikans of brandy would upset the operation. The men were in no mood for another fiasco such as the one experienced in the last raid. Every man kept a wary eye on his companions.

Out of the tropical blackness the almost invisible form of

a Cimarrone slipped up alongside the raider's leader to inform him the train was coming. The word was passed along to each man in line as they hid alongside the trail. Soon the tinkle of brass mule bells was heard, softly breaking the silence of the humid night air.

It was almost morning light when the lead mule hove out of the gloom and into sight. Appearing somewhat like a ghostly dragon emerging from a wall of jungle, the animal train moved down the trail. The caravan was a large one. There were one hundred ninety mules in all, with forty-five guards. Once more the shrill whistle pierced the silence and the trap was sprung. There was only a brief exchange of shots and arrows before the treasure guards retreated into the forest. As was expected, being so close to the end of their journey, the convoy protectors had become lax in their vigilance and were taken completely unawares. Drake, with the larger force and the advantage of surprise, plus having the aid of the Cimarrones who the Spanish much feared, routed the Iberians almost at once. Some of the treasure defenders circled the raiders and ran toward town, yelling loudly for reinforcements.

The invaders set about stripping the mules of their precious cargo at a feverish pace. Each pack was dumped on the ground to ascertain its contents, for gold was the most desired metal in preference to the just as heavy silver plate. Merchandise of any kind was desired even less than the silver. Fifteen tons of silver plate and bars were on the train. Most of this the freebooters endeavored to hide in nearby land crab holes, under the roots of trees, and in depressions scooped out of the earth by hand. Time was short. It would be only a little while longer before the town's garrison would be alerted by the mule train guards. Because of this, the silver was poorly hidden.

Drake and Le Testu pressed the men to hurry. Their instructions were to load themselves first with gold and jewels, then, if they could carry silver, all right. But there was no time to waste. Pursuing Spanish soldiers would not be burdened with cumbersome packs. Time was just as valuable as gold.

The difficult trek back to the river mouth was one of complete exhaustion for the men. Each raider was loaded beyond his capacity for an easy carry. Gold and greed have always been a partnership for men. The dense jungle, with swamp-covered areas, was a hard trek to make burdened with the heavy gold. To add to the difficulty of the human pack animals, it began to rain in torrents. The packs themselves added to their discomfort, for the bundles were makeshift and difficult to carry. Most were leather bags tied two-together and slung over the shoulder, an extremely cumbersome and unwieldy method of carrying a heavy burden.

When the exhausted band finally reached the Rio San Francisco, the pinnaces were not at the rendezvous site! The disappointment and frustration was overwhelming. All the men were worn out and some were wounded. In fact, Captain Le Testu, the French shipmaster, had been wounded in the stomach and was left behind, guarded by a pair of his crew. Until the end of the trek, little thought had been given to the hard work and injuries suffered because of the apparently successful acquisition of wealth for all. But waiting on the shore, Spanish soldiers probably close at their heels, and the apparent failure of their comrades to carry out their obligation with the pinnaces, the men began to curse.

Drake was not the type of leader to allow misfortune to disrupt the success of the venture. Scouts were sent out to look for the missing boats. Soon returning, they reported more bad news. A small flotilla of Spanish sloops had been sighted just off shore, apparently heading for Nombre de Dios. The gloom spread among Drake's men. The Spaniards must have captured the pinnaces, perhaps they had even found the frigate and overpowered it.

But Drake, always confident, was not convinced. If the frigate had been captured, it would have been with the sloops. The practical thing to do was to remain calm, set out guards to protect the camp, and proceed to construct a raft so the pinnaces could be searched for.

Work and hope are always the defeaters of despair. With renewed will, the men set about to build a raft. Small tree trunks were lashed together, a makeshift mast with a just as makeshift sail was installed. Drake and three seamen jumped aboard. As the half-awash platform moved into the stream, Drake waved to the company left behind and yelled, "If it please God that I shall ever set foot aboard my frigate in safety I will, God willing, by one means or another, get you all aboard in spite of all the Spaniards in the Indies."

The words were typical of Drake. He never gave up.

GOLDEN HINDE

Postscript #1
Francis Drake Northwest

Reprinted from Collector's Pamphlet No.5, "Francis Drake Northwest," copyright 1978 by Donald M. Viles and Charlene Viles.

Perhaps the most puzzling maritime mystery in the record of the world is the track of Francis Drake in 1579 when he was on the West Coast of North America. Speculation as to where he had been began as soon as Drake returned to England from his globe-circling voyage.

During the past four centuries many books have been published about Drake's voyage and more are still being readied for the press. Perhaps the two best known volumes are *The World Encompassed*, by Sir Francis Drake (the mariner's nephew) produced in the seventeenth century, and *Sir Francis Drake's Voyage Around the World*, by Henry Wagner, produced in the twentieth century. *World Encompassed* was pure propaganda prepared by England to taunt Spain, England's foremost enemy at the time. *Voyage Around The World* was an ambitious scholarly attempt to compile in one volume all that was known about Drake's voyage. As a reference, Wagner's book is beyond comparison. However, as a solution to the mystery of Drake's 1579 trek, it failed completely.

During the past decade, several theories have been put forth as to the place on the Northwest Coast of North America where the English sea captain careened his famous ship the *Golden Hinde* for repairs. Several areas in and about today's San Francisco Bay have been chosen as the site. All designations have been far off course, their supporters being victims of Tudor England's propaganda security measures.

***

Francis Drake made a voyage around the globe that began in England in December 1577 and ended back at those famous isles in 1580. It was the first known circumnavigation in which the beginning captain was at the helm when the vessel returned to its starting place. Drake's voyage was also noteworthy because it was the first time an English ship challenged the authority of Spain in the Pacific Ocean, a sea so well occupied by the Iberians that it had become known as the "Spanish Lake."

The globe-traversing trip was the forerunner of many English voyages in the Pacific that would bid defiance to the Spanish domination. Gold and silver from the mines of North and South America lured many mariners to the western side of the world. However, a ship's cargo of treasure was only a small bit of loot compared to the largest prize of all, the ownership of the new lands.

Francis Drake's voyage has always been one of mystery. Historians have been able to trace the course of the *Golden Hinde* (ex-*Pelican*) until it reached the west coasts of South and North America. But once arriving, the ship's exact locations are unknown. After leaving these coasts, the track of the ship again became clear. Other mysteries were also connected with the voyage.

The stocky, red-bearded Drake captured a Spanish vessel and relieved it of its cargo of gold and silver. For this, some scholars labeled the daring mariner a pirate. Pirate he was not. England and Spain had been waging undeclared war for years. When Drake returned to England, he delivered his cargo to Queen Elizabeth I. The gold and silver procurement was only a small act in a long and ferocious drama between England and Spain.

Spain was carrying on a fast-spreading occupation of North America in the latter years of the sixteenth century. Her goal was to occupy the greater part of the continent before other European nations could challenge her with their own conquests. The Spanish used every means possible to defeat their enemies. False maps were drawn up and deliberately placed in the hands of the foe. Spurious records were also distributed and made available to their adversaries.

Sixteenth century documents, falsified for national security, and complicated political intrigues of subsequent centuries are the two reasons why Drake's track along the

west coast of North America has never be resolved.
    Before Queen Elizabeth I sent Francis Drake on the voyage, no accurate knowledge was available concerning Spanish operations on America's Pacific Coast. Spanish documents stated locations as being far different than the information English espionage agents gleaned from spies and travelers. There is no doubt but that the primary purpose of Drake's voyage was to clarify what the Spanish were doing and where. His chore was to chart the coastline and harbors with precise scientific data.
    Captain James Cook, in the eighteenth century, has always been given credit for English maritime exploration on the American western coast, but it was Francis Drake, 200 years earlier, who had compiled the data for Cook to follow. Francis Drake was an unsung scientific explorer because of political necessity. Cook received the praise by reason of the same obligement. Both men were dedicated servants of their country.
    Drake carried with him several "artisans." Today we call them surveyors, astronomers, and mathematicians. As the *Golden Hinde* plied her way along the west coast, Drake's nephew, an accomplished artist, painted pictures of the coastline. Channels were sounded for depth and the sun continually "shot" to determine latitude location. There is evidence that the width of the North American continent was also determined through celestial observations. Drake's crew compiled the first *Coast Pilot*, a book of directions for mariners in the English language. Some modern writers have claimed that this important book was given to Queen Elizabeth I, but then lost. Such a statement is ridiculous. England has never been careless with important records; in fact it has a world reputation for saving everything for posterity. So it undoubtedly the first *Coast Pilot* remains in safe keeping with the rest of the records concerning Francis Drake. A small slip in English security during the eighteenth century revealed that mariner George Vancouver found it necessary to consult Drake's records. Another English sea captain, James Colnett, was also familiar with the Tudor mariner's work.

For some obscure reason, land-oriented people are prone to consider marine scientific data as sacred and always true. If a mariner states he was in a specific degree of latitude, his integrity is never questioned. Perhaps it is thought a sailor wouldn't dare falsify such an important thing as latitude, or surely he would wreck his ship. Such thinking is ludicrous. Seamen are some of the best liars in the world. They can only be outdone by politicians. When one considers that Francis Drake was the world's best seaman at the time, and Queen Elizabeth I was the best of all politicians, then surely these two could concoct the finest of falsehoods. They did. And now marks over 400 years that historians have been swallowing these lies.

Spain started the spurious latitude declarations on the West Coast of North America. England countered with same when releasing information about Drake's trip. Colima, California, River of the Firebrands, Bay of Fire, and the Strait of Anian were all places shrouded in Spanish mystery. These sites were also some of the places that Drake set out to locate and chart. When the mariner returned home, England produced spurious documents to match those of the Spanish so that Spain could not be certain where Drake went. Political intrigue piled upon political intrigue.

In Drake record, some of the latitudes were falsified by twenty degrees. Thus, when it was documented that the *Golden Hinde* was beached in a small harbor in thirty-eight degrees North Latitude, the actual location of the careening was in fifty-eight degrees North Latitude.

Historians have dredged up all sorts of excuses and reasons for freezing weather off the coast of Oregon during the month of June in order to justify a statement in the Drake papers. But this is a falsified latitude. Drake was in today's Bering Sea, and the weather was indeed freezing.

The *Golden Hinde* was a sturdy vessel. She had a double-planked hull for working in the ice and carried several large guns for protection. The ship was so well armed and the Spanish ships in the Pacific so poorly protected, that the English intrusion was comparable to dropping a tiger into a flock of sheep. From the Iberians Drake faced only one major danger. While surveying the coastline, if he placed the *Hinde* in narrow or land-bound waterways, conceivably the ship could be surrounded by small boats and boarded. But given sea-room, the vessel was a formidable warship. The danger of capture was greatest when the vessel was careened for repairs.

In 1579 Francis Drake sailed the *Golden Hinde* up the west coast of today's United States and Canada as far as the Arctic Ocean. After satisfying the charting needs of his country, he reversed his course for a distance and then headed for the China Seas and home.

North America is a land with 350 years of totally spurious record; a record put forth to this day as "heritage." Documents have always been tools in the hands of political leaders. When the continent of North America was a conquest prize for all of Europe, political intrigue and the security of nations dictated the necessity of document manipulation. Because of the length of time required to settle the first European ownership of the continent, false records became so numerous, and were given so much credibility, that there was no manner in which they could be successfully repudiated. Today, the tools are available to straighten out the falsehoods, but we are so brainwashed that we have lost all desire for truth.

The spurious record of Francis Drake was only a very small segment of North America's fake records, yet it dramatically illustrates the effect of written and printed word manipulation. World famous historians and scholars have studied the mariner's sea-track for many decades, only to erroneously reach the same conclusions channeled for them by Queen Elizabeth I and her advisors 400 years ago.

STRAIT OF ANIAN

Supposedly a mythical strait because of falsified latitudes in various documents, but Francis Drake sailed the *Golden Hinde* through this waterway to verify its existence. In all probability, the sea track went as far as the ice pack, which was probably at about sixty-eight degrees. In later years, the straight was called Strait of Juan de Fuca but is now called the Bering Strait in honor of a man who didn't discover it. The rock that juts out of the sea in this straight was dubbed "Pillar of Hercules" by Fuca, but it is now called Fairway Rock.

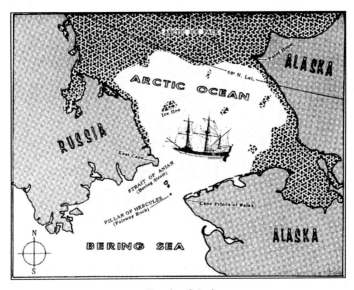

Strait of Anian

DRAKE'S BAY

A counterfeit record engraved on a slab of brass has been used to identify today's San Francisco Bay in California as the port where Francis Drake careened the ship *Golden Hinde* for repairs. North of San Francisco a stone cross has been set up as a marker to commemorate the landing and a coastline dent has been named Drake's Bay. Also at this location, a sand-plugged sea arm has been designated Drake's Estero. Further north, Bodega Bay has been deemed by some as the proper landing site.

The little cover in which Francis Drake chose to repair his ship still bears the name of the famous mariner. Oddly enough, it is now the Spanish epithet for Drake that survives. The Iberians called him "Devil Drake" or *el Diablo*. Devil's Cove, on the eastern side of the Alaska Peninsula, in fifty-eight degrees, twenty-one minutes North Latitude is the true Drake's Bay.

In Drake's records there are descriptions of the area where the *Hinde* was overhauled. It says there were "trees without leaves" and "white banks and cliffs." He says the natives called out, "Hiyoh" to the ship's crew. At Devil's Cove there are trees without leaves and white banks and cliffs, for this is the glacier-strewn Land of Ten Thousand Smokes where fantastic volcanic action has periodically killed the trees and left volcanic ash in great banks.

Just north of Devil's Cove is Hallo Bay, undoubtedly another surviving recognition of Drake's visit.

Francis Drake was not the first European mariner to view the Alaska Peninsula. Thirty-seven years earlier, Juan Cabrillo sighted the area and stopped near the same location. He called his landing place Baia de los Fuegos (Bay of Fires).

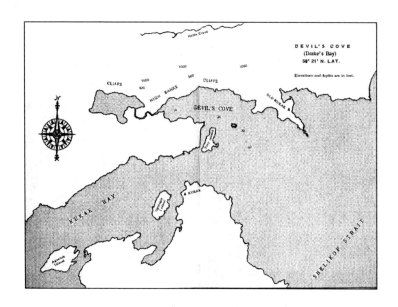

Devil's Cove (Drake's Bay) 58° 21' N. Latitude

Port New Albion

On a sixteenth century map, known as the Hondius Broadside, is a small drawing depicting the bay where Drake careened the *Golden Hinde* in the north. The drawing shows what appears to be people standing by campfires. People standing by a fire is too commonplace for such an important drawing, so it is more likely that the depiction represents either natives or English sailors warming themselves by steaming fumeroles.

Whether it is called Land of Ten Thousand Smokes, or the Baja de los Fuegos, it means the same thing—a place where thousands of volcanic jets of steam puff up through the ground. Some of the mud flat areas around the bays give the appearance of gigantic pots of puffing and blowing porridge.

Images from 16th century Hondius map showing volcanic steam vents puffing out of harbor mud, behind the *Golden Hinde*.

Colnett's Map

English mariner James Colnett gained a placed in history when he was detained by the Spanish at the northwest port of Nootka in 1789. The records of Colnett's voyage contain a map of Drake's Bay. Government cartographers made little change in the original work, other than connecting Tiny Island with the mainland and inserting a false mileage scale. In Colnett's record, twenty degrees of latitude was dropped from the harbor's location, thus locating Drake's Bay at thirty-eight degrees, twenty-one minutes North Latitude. Its true location is fifty-eight degrees, twenty-one minutes North Latitude.

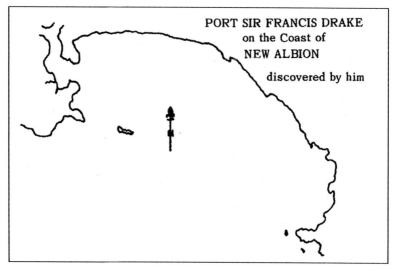

Facsimile of map produced for James Colnett record during voyage of *Argonaut*, April 26, 1789 to November 3, 1791.

ISLAND OF CALIFORNIA

Seventeenth century cartographers had a difficult time depicting western North America. English and Spanish propaganda, mixed with waterfront gleanings and other information made it impossible to sort truth from fiction. The result of their questions and endeavors was a map that portrayed California as a huge island stretching along fifteen hundred miles of coastline. However, the shape given to the island conforms correctly and indicates the cartographers had received some truthful information.

Modern cartographic experts and historians point to the Island of California as a piece of geographical misconception dreamed up by early cartographers. But the joke is on contemporary experts. Queen Elizabeth I and her advisors believed California was an island. Francis Drake sailed around it to prove this fact. That California was surrounded by water was not news to the Spanish; they had known California was an island since it was discovered by Hernan Cortez. But to have other countries discover this was something the Spanish were not happy about. The circumnavigation of California by Drake created consternation among the Iberians because keeping secret the geographic locations of their operations was so important. The Spanish began an intensive propaganda program to discredit the English mariner's reports as soon as he returned to England. The Spanish depicted California as a peninsula both by words and by cartography. The expostulations had no effect on the seventeenth century English statesmen, but the world in general has been effectively convinced.

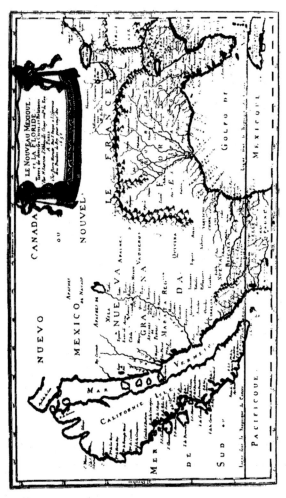

New Mexico and Florida, showing the Island of California, 1656

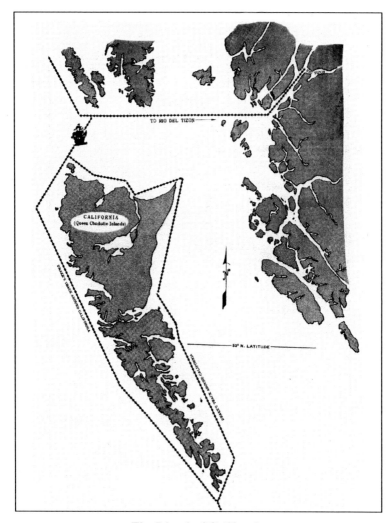

The Island of California

RIO DEL TIZON

Called the Rio del Tizon (River of Firebrands) by the Spanish because a river of molten lava flowed into the waterway, this stream was an important checkpoint for the English mariner. Francis Drake probably conned the *Golden*

Hinde into Portland Inlet and went as far as the mouth of the Rio del Tizon (now called the Nass River).

Spain endeavored to camouflage the name of the river by stating that the stream had been given its name because natives living along its banks carried hot coals next to their stomachs to keep warm. It is evident the English were not swayed by these crude cover-up attempts. Francis Drake undoubtedly identified the Rio del Tizon because of the great quantity of lava and cinders deposited at the river's mouth. Tizons are porous, light and buoyant cinders and lava.

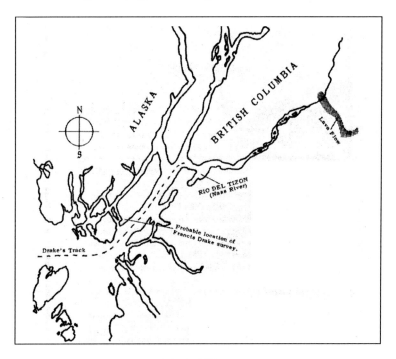

Rio Del Tizon

DRAKE'S TRACK

Necessity dictated that Drake's track hang close to the west coast of North America because his voyage was primarily for gain of scientific knowledge. Consequently, to accurately draw and paint the contours of headlands and other points conducive to recognition by subsequent English mariners, the *Golden Hinde* sailed within a few miles of shore. At various degrees of latitude, the course was altered and the ship hove to in order for crews to go ashore to take star sights and make plane table surveys for proof of visit or territorial claims. Archeological and documentary indications are that landings were made at 35 degrees, 45 degrees, 55 degrees, and 60 degrees North Latitude on Pacific shores. Quite probably claims of title were made on the Bering Sea and Arctic coasts of Alaska as well. Drake spent considerable time repairing the *Golden Hinde* at fifty-eight degrees North Latitude. It is the author's belief that during this period the mariner would have sent out exploration parties in small boats, and thus would have investigated Cook's Inlet. The track indicated around Nunivak is one any curious mariner would make if opportunity presented. The circular track in the Arctic Ocean indicates a route to check shorelines as far as the ice pack.

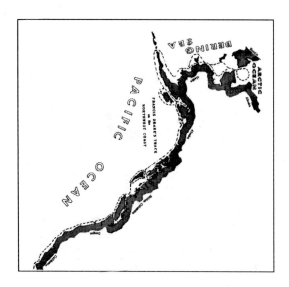

Drake's Track - California to the Arctic Circle

POSTSCRIPT #2
NORTH AMERICA'S HIDDEN LEGACY AT NEAH-KAH-NIE MOUNTAIN
1579

Reprinted from Hidden Heritage Series, North America Historiography, copyright 1982 by Donald M. Viles.

This record of search for the truth of Neah-Kah-Nie Mountain's famous mystery has been a two-stage affair. The first stage was conducted over a two-year period, 1969 to 1971, when the author and Mr. Wayne Jensen, Jr. conducted a program of platting and ground search which revealed that the marked stones of the Neah-Kah-Nie could only be the result of a land survey made by Francis Drake in 1579. Irrefutable proof of the survey deduction was not to be found at that time. However, the author pursued the quest of verification for another decade. The final pieces of the puzzle did not reveal themselves until autumn of this year.

—Donald M. Viles
October 1981

THE MOUNTAIN

Neah-Kah-Nie Mountain is a prominent headland on the west coast of North America, jutting into the Pacific Ocean at approximately forty-five degrees, 45 minutes North Latitude, on the central Oregon coast.

It is an outstanding point, with towering, rugged basalt cliffs at the sea's edge, backed up on the east side by a high ridge of land. It stands above all other areas of the coastline for hundreds of miles on either side. A modern highway has been chiseled deep into the rock sides of the mountain, affording travelers a spectacular view of the Pacific and nearby headlands.

A few years after the end of the Mexican War one of the first settlers of the mountain area discovered several huge stones engraved with strange symbols. It was obvious from the first that the marks were the work of man and not the result of natural causes. The stones were found at the base of the mountain, on its south side, close to the ocean beach.

About two miles south of this location lay the scattered bones of a teak-built sailing ship. Some of the ship's cargo, huge slabs of beeswax, was scattered about in the nearby sands.

With their imaginations operating at a high pitch, several local people immediately deduced that a ship built of teakwood had to be of Spanish origin and that in all probability the rocks marked the way to a buried treasure hidden by pirates!

The mountain is now pockmarked with treasure-seeking excavations, some of them quite deep, bearing proof of the faith and determination of men seeking riches. Other diggings are small and shallow, the difficult removal of the rocky soil apparently deterring treasure seekers.

For more than a century the search for the treasure of Neah-Kah-Nie has been ongoing. For sundry reasons, there has always been a considerable amount of digging executed after dark. Some searchers worked in secrecy because their fear of "claim jumpers" who might dig a little deeper and make off with the hoard while the owners of the excavation were taking a needed rest. In later years, some of the search area has been turned into an Oregon State Park. With this advent, working in the dark became even more prevalent in order to avoid the entanglement of official permits demanded by State officials intent upon keeping park tourists safe from falling into treasure pits.

A Different Search

In 1969 the author deduced that the strange glyphs on the "treasure rocks" were not simple direction marks, but were instead compass bearings or "rays." Working on this premise, a program of graphic projection and physical search began. A request to participate in the ground searches, extending from the draftings, was accepted by Mr. Wayne Jensen, Jr., an archeologist and collector of published articles concerning Neah-Kah-Nie.

The primary requisite for initiating the search was to determine the exact original position of the so-called Treasure Rocks. Since their discovery, these stones had been moved several times to accommodate various building projects and other land changes. When the site location was determined, measurements were taken of the angles in the "rays" engraved on the stones and then charts were drawn.

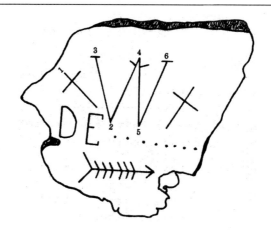

Treasure Rock (Figure 1)

This set of marks was found on one of the stones discovered by early settlers at Neah-Kah-Nie Mountain. The stone was close to the ocean beach, on the south side of the mountain. The "W" and the crosses are compass bearings. "DE" means "distance east" and the dots represent distance in that direction one must go to locate the next triangulation station. This showstone had a small amount of vandalism, but not enough to eliminate its value.

The dots represented approximately 100 yards per dot. Sixteenth century surveyors were quite exclusive with their work and were not willing to share their plats with others in the trade. Using dots to represent distance was a method used by William Bourne. By this means, the scale of a survey triangulation would be known only to the one who knew the scale of the dots.

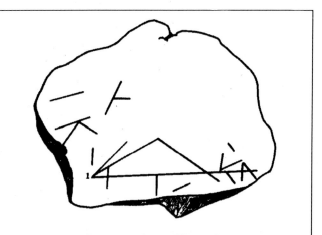

Treasure Rock (Figure 2)

This showstone was found at the same location as the Treasure Rock in Figure 1. At the time of its fabrication, the marks were probably quite elaborate but during the first part of the twentieth century, pranksters apparently wanted to make the stone appear to be the work of Pat Smith, an early treasure hunter. Originally, the stone may have shown most of the main triangulation compass directions. The long line at the bottom represented an east-west bearing, with this stone being at position 1 in the drawing.

The first productive physical search was undertaken by the author after the first angle plotting was made. This plotting and search revealed a cliff face that had engraved in its surface many marks that were later to prove a magnificent record of an English territory claim, made in 1579 by the great mariner Francis Drake for Queen Elizabeth I of Tudor England.

Augur Rock, as it was dubbed for reference, was chiseled with measurements for two survey baselines—one on the magnetic meridian, and the other at an angle to the magnetic meridian. These measurements were illustrated by Roman numerals: MEVM, and CMM. MEVM proved to be the meridian baseline measurement and CMM was a measure for a baseline projecting easterly from Augur Rock. The cliff face was given the name Augur Rock because more deeply engraved than the other marks was the word "AUGUR," which means "Interpretation."

Augur Rock in 1969

When originally marked in 1579, this stone face apparently had the entire triangulation story of the survey incised in its surface. In this photo, the marks were chalked in for photographic purposes. The marks were most easily seen when the sun struck the rock face at an angle, which created a shadow in the grooves.

Above the word "AUGUR", and connected to it by a looping line, was a graph, or gridwork, later to be identified as a survey triangulation symbol. Illustrations of the main angles in the survey plat were also engraved. And incised in the basalt rock was a secret, provable record of the date when the engravings were made. This set of carvings was in the form of three uncial letters—EEM.

Many of the marks on the cliff were quite faint. The savage sou'wester winter storms of the Oregon Coast, with their driving rains, had slowly but steadily eroded the hard rock face through the centuries. Some of the glyphs could be seen only in the morning or afternoon hours when the sun's rays would strike the grooves at an angle. Undoubtedly there were marks that had disappeared entirely.

Augur Rock Mark Explanation

EEM, the letters at the upper left, represent star sights taken on a particular night to identify date of sight. MEVM is the Roman numeral measurement of the meridian baseline. CMM, in the lower left corner, is the Roman numeral equivalent of a baseline bearing eastward from this cliff. Some of the remaining marks are triangulation marks, and others, like the group of short vertical lines, have not been deciphered.

At the time of the cliff discovery, the carvings on Augur Rock were a mystery. There was no clue then regarding measurement units and no known measurement unit with which to work. At that point in the search the author was working on the theory that the rocks, marked with compass bearings, represented a cross-bearing plotting to a cached ship's cargo, probably left by the stranded crew of the wrecked teakwood sailing vessel.

When it was deduced that the Roman numerals on Augur Rock were measurement glyphs, plottings were drawn using the Spanish measurement of Pie, or foot, which was equal to about eleven English inches. Use of this measurement was influenced by the belief that the wrecked teak-built ship was Spanish, and that if a cargo had been cached, it would have been placed close to the ocean beach for easy reloading. Many plottings were drawn and many ground searches made, all with a complete lack of success.

Much of the ground search included the use of metal

detectors. Fisher Research Laboratories in Palo Alto, California, contributed to the search program by donating two shallow-scanning metal detectors to compliment the deep-probe machine of their manufacture that was already in use.

When the author's wife suggested the use of the Spanish Vara as a unit of measure in the chart making, this thought was acceded to, as all other work with the Pie measure had produced nothing. Very little optimism was accorded the Vara measure, as this placed platted cross-bearings far up the mountainside, which was certainly no place to bury a ship's cargo.

The Spanish Vara is of different lengths, designated according to the particular area of the world where it is used. So three plottings were drafted, each using a different length Vara as the unit of measure. By this time, another marked stone had been deciphered and another measurement decoded. This stone was given the name "Wendle's Rock" in reference to the man who discovered it many years ago (see page 131).

With the use of the decoded marks of Augur Rock and Wendle's Rock, and using the Vara as a measurement unit, the plotting encompassed more than a square mile of land! To embrace such a large area for the project did not seem plausible at the time, but a ground search was undertaken. Immediate results were produced.

A large stone platform was found, marking the apex of a triangulation A momentous discovery followed—a boulder engraved with several marks, resting within a triangle of stones. Also found was a large stone that had a deeply incised angle on its surface. This boulder was dubbed "Wayne's Rock" for the man who found it (see page 132).

I then realized the "Treasure Rocks" of Neah-Kah-Nie were marks of a land survey. This was the only feasible conclusion in light of what had been found. The mystery then became deeper. Who could possibly have surveyed the Oregon Coast in ancient times?

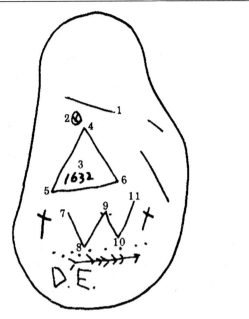

Wendle's Rock

Wendle's Rock was found a few hundred feet from the ocean beach. It is a large stone, smooth and rounded by years of tumbling in the sea's surf. Drake's surveyors carried it to its site at the south end of the measured meridian baseline where it was placed on a large mound of stones. The dots are units of measurement and "DE" means "Distance East."

Another discovery of major importance came next. Plotting had pinpointed an area where a ground mark should show the north end of the meridian baseline. This spot was discovered after a short search. At that location was a major key to the survey—a stone carved to illustrate the unit of measure used in laying out the survey. It was an English yard!

Of the three different lengths of the Spanish Vara used in the search map plottings, the Valencia Vara, which is 35.90 English inches, was the measurement unit that led to finding the north termination point of the meridian baseline. This is an obscure and seldom-used Spanish measure, which was probably derived from the English yard.

Wayne's Rock – Stone Triangle

Wayne's Rock has a deeply incised angle mark in its surface. This rock was located shortly after the plotting and finding of a stone triangle at the north end of the measured mile. The angle denotes the meridian line and a bearing line westward and south from is location. The Stone Triangle is a structure of stones outlining a triangle shape. Within this border of rocks was a large stone with a single line engraved on its surface. The Stone Triangle, with its showrocks, marked the north end of what William Bourne called the Vin Yard Mile, or a mile proven in length by measuring by the yard. In the photo, the Stone Triangle is surrounded by white compass bearing photo indicators. The arrow sits atop Wayne's Rock, which has the incised angle chalked in for photo purposes.

With proof of the triangle apex measurement glyph on Wendle's Rock, and the measurement glyphs on Augur Rock, there was no doubt about what was marked on the rocks of Neah-Kah-Nie Mountain. The rocks were evidence of an English survey. As the first engraved stones discovered were found by the original Anglo-American settlers in the area, and the stone marks were obviously quite old, the question as to who executed the land measurement became a deep puzzle. There was no known historical record of a survey having been made by England, yet the evidence was beyond question that one had been executed.

Research began to indicate that the survey had been rendered by Francis Drake in 1579, but this deduction could still not be sufficiently proven so the project was terminated.

ANOTHER QUEST AND REVELATION

Although a ground search of Neah-Kah-Nie was no longer needed, the tantalizing question remained as to why there was no record of Francis Drake making a land survey on the west coast of North America.

Ten years of tedious research has revealed the answer: political maneuvering!

When the ownership of North America was contested by England, Spain, France and the United States, it best served the purpose of politics that the survey not be revealed. The research has also irrefutably disclosed that the survey had been engineered by Francis Drake and his company during the years 1577 to 1580.

Drake's "official" record of his visit to the west coast of North America during his circumnavigation has always been an enigma to historians. The documents of the voyage are quite jumbled and it is obvious they are not accurate. Now, with the discovery and proving of the Neah-Kah-Nie Survey, a new chapter has been added to the famous mariner's record. This chapter reveals the track of Drake on the Pacific coast.

Francis Drake signed both England's and his own name to the Neah-Kah-Nie Survey and territory claim. It was not a signature of English alphabet letters spelling out D-R-A-K-E, but instead it was a series of mathematical signatures that could only have been placed by him.

The survey is a plane-table triangulation based on the methods introduced primarily by Leonard Digges and William Bourne in the sixteenth century. Leonard Digges was a mathematician and the first Englishman to produce a book on surveying written in simplified terms. *A Booke Named Tectonicon* was published in 1556 and it explained how to use mathematical triangulation in the measuring of land.

William Bourne, a student of Digges' methods, extended the teachings of Digges by producing a printed treatise on the use of mathematics in navigation. Bourne's work, following his teacher's example, was executed in the simplest terms possible so that seamen with only a minimal education might use it. Bourne's book, *A Regiment For The Sea*, was carried by Drake on his circumnavigation voyage. The Neah-Kah-Nie Survey is a copy of Bourne's methods, so it is deduced that Drake either carried other works by William Bourne, or that the surveyors with Drake had been schooled by the English mathematician.

It is evident that the Drake survey was a pre-determined English territory claim method by which all possible means were executed to assure permanence and proof. This claim was a plane-table survey of super-deluxe quality. A standard land measurement of this type would have a few stacked-up stone mounds to mark important points of baselines, and then all other marks would be on paper only. But this is not the case with Neah-Kah-Nie. On this mountain there were many stone mounds marking various points of the triangulation and dozens of engraved stones. Each important line crossing of the triangulations was chiseled in stone and placed on the ground in its proper position. For each mark and crossing on the surveyor's plane-table chart, was a corresponding mark placed on the land, engraved in stone.

This was apparently a secret survey. At no single location was all the information in place that would be needed to trace out the triangulation claim. In Drake's time, and until modern day, it would have been impossible for a stranger to the Neah-Kah-Nie land measurement to trace out the plat. The unit of measure was not noted at the same location where baseline measurements were placed. These allied and extremely important marks were more than a mile apart! It was only because of access to modern air photos and modern transportation that the survey secret was revealed. Also, most fortunate, was the chart plotting by Valencia Vara.

Francis Drake's territory claim survey would have withstood any onslaught by Spanish or other who might wish to destroy it. True, some markers could be carried off or ruined, but dozens of others would have remained because of the impossibility of locating them. Exemplary of this are the many treasure hunters who endeavored to decode and follow marks on rocks they found.

If political need had seen fit for Queen Elizabeth I (or any later English monarch) to prove that a claim had been made, it would have been a simple matter. England could have shown the charted survey on paper and the marks of the crucial points of measure to any nation's diplomats. They could have corroborated their claim at the survey site, by indicating the same marks, carved in stone, on the land.

One of the most important segments of evidence was engraved at Augur Rock. If it had been necessary for England to prove that Drake had left a record, the coded date incised in the cliff could not have been disputed. Elizabeth's surveyors recorded the transit of three fixed stars as proof of date by chiseling a code, used only by William Bourne, into the cliff face.

Many of the Drake Survey marks were lost before the Neah-Kah-Nie mystery was solved. Treasure excavations and souvenir collectors took some away. A triangulation site on the east side of the survey was lost due to logging. The south end of the meridian baseline was destroyed by housing and development encroachment, but fortunately the owner of the land preserved the marker stone he found atop the rock mound (Wendle's Rock). And by pure good fortune, the monument mound at the north end of the meridian baseline was still intact at the time of the survey ground search.

The original "Treasure Rocks" and Wendle's Rock are now at the Tillamook county Pioneer Museum in Tillamook, Oregon. Francis Drake's land claim at Neah-Kah-Nie Mountain is the key to a vast hidden record of North America and is of inestimable value to future generations.

Unfortunately, the political heads of the State of Oregon have never seen fit to embrace the research of Neah-Kah-Nie's mystery. At the time of this printing, what is undoubtedly the most important historical site in North America and the world's most important historical survey remains unmarked and unheralded.

TRIANGULATION SURVEY BY WILLIAM BOURNE

The triangulation plat shown on the next page is a survey executed by William Bourne, at Gravesend, near London, England, in the later part of the sixteenth century. Bourne's dot system of measurement units is illustrated at the upper left. He denotes it, *"The skell or tronk of mesur,"* or "The scale or trunk of measure." This is the same illustration of measurement scale used by Francis Drake at the Neah-Kah-Nie survey. Also, Drake used the dot illustration at other points his voyage.

Top right, indicates the end of the measured mile as *"Vin Yard Myll,"* or "a proven mile measured in yards." The Vin Yard Myll point is at the angle of the triangulation. In all probability, the measured mile of this survey had the same type of marked stone as the one found on Neah-Kah-Nie.

This illustration of Bourne's triangulation was published in 1578. It is the first understandable public printing of triangulation surveying. This new style of land measurement was brought to light the year following Drake's departure on his circumnavigation voyage.

English political and security representatives were not reticent in casting printed barbs at their adversaries, the Spanish. Bourne's book was titled *Treasure For Travelers,* normally an unlikely title, if it were not that both Spain and England were extremely interested in the most important treasure of the time, North America. It is probable that William Bourne was a member of the Drake expedition and traveling under the alias "Francis Fletcher." Bourne's stepson was one of the group accompanying Martin Frobisher to Newfoundland and it is within the realm of probability that either he or his stepfather, or both of them, embarked on the Drake expedition. It was a practice in those times for a person to make out a will before embarking on a dangerous journey. William Bourne made his will in 1573; an indication of journeying to far places. Bourne died in 1582.

A number of years after Drake's return to England an "official" record of his voyage was published. Notably, much of the record was taken from notes by Francis Fletcher and it was printed for a Mr. Bourne. The first line, in italics, in the first paragraph of this document asks the question, *"Whose land survey you?"* After more than four hundred years, silent stones of the ancient triangulation survey on Neah-Kah-Nie Mountain cry out loudly in the voice of a stocky red-haired mariner, *"This land is claimed for England, measured by Bourne."*

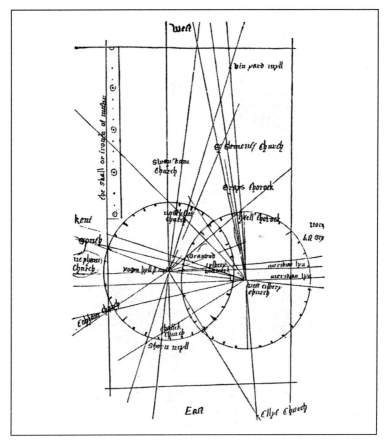

A Triangulation Survey by William Bourne

SURVEY AT NEAH-KAH-NIE
FRANCIS DRAKE - WILLIAM BOURNE

Some of the survey lines in the figure below were printed in bold to show the "W" on Treasure Rock No. 1 and the triangle on Wendle's Rock. Fortunately, for posterity, the main triangulation marks of the Drake-Bourne survey at Neah-Kah-Nie managed to elude land developers, loggers, and treasure hunters until they were deciphered. However, some marked stones have been lost forever.

Some secondary triangulations were made west of Augur Rock. These calculations were made along the edge of the mountain as far north as Short Sands Beach. Much treasure hunting was conducted in this area after the survey markers were found.

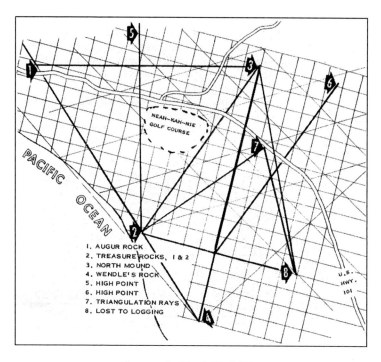

Survey At Neah-Kah-Nie

Francis Drake's Voyage

Francis Drake made the first circumnavigation of the world in which the same captain was at the helm of the ship from start to finish. His trip was one of secrecy due to the competition among European nations claiming sections of North America. England, under the leadership of Queen Elizabeth I, was on the threshold of becoming a world power. The island nation was embracing a program of science in the fields of navigation and land measurement, an undertaking that in later years would contribute to taken command of the world's seas. Drake's voyage was one of exploration, trade, and science.

In 1577, when Francis Drake began his voyage, mathematics for land and sea had only made its debut for the average man. Martin Frobisher had just returned to England from a voyage in which he executed a land survey territory claim in the Newfoundland area. In 1577, it was Drake's turn, and later, another English mariner named Humphrey Gilbert, would measure a piece of North America for claim rights.

All these voyages were made under a veil of strict security, for their purpose was to make solid, indisputable territory claims on the continent of North America. Spain had already made inroads on the land, as had France. But England's adversaries had not made provable claims in the realm of international law. The Spanish would erect a cross in newly explored territory, recite a few prayers, and throw handfuls of grass to the four winds as their method of claim. These claims were strictly ceremonial and certainly not provable events. The French rarely bothered with any type of formal claiming, other than stating a record of exploration.

In the contest for the North American continent, Spain employed a documentary ruse to divert other nations from the areas of her explorations. By royal decree, all records concerning North America had to be approved by the Spanish government before they could be published or shown publicly. Making use of this law for security purposes, Spanish censors changed latitudes of locations in various records and then deliberately deployed them to the English and other European adversaries. An example of this deception is in the "official" record of the voyage of Juan Cabrillo in 1540. According to documents handed down to modern generations, Cabrillo sailed up the west coast of North America as far as forty-two degrees North Latitude. The latitude stated in this record was faked—Juan Cabrillo actually sailed as far north as the Bering Sea of the west coast of today's Alaska. The Spanish changed the latitude in an effort to deceive other nations regarding Spain's whereabouts in western North America. The reason was to induce other country's explorers, who might be trying to locate Spanish claims, to waste time searching in the wrong areas. This ploy was to help Spain gain time for colonization in distant places.

Such a secret is hard to keep, especially among seamen, and rumors of true location of Spanish voyages reached back to England. Francis Drake was chosen to sail to the west coast of North America, search out the geographic truth of Spanish activity, and most important of all, make a land claim north of the highest latitude of Spanish claims. It was political intrigue at its best. The furthest point north that the spurious Spanish claimed was at forty-two degrees, and this latitude designation was used against them.

Francis Drake carried out his mission. He executed a provable scientific land claim at Neah-Kah-Nie Mountain, just four degrees north of the falsified Spanish claim. Spain's ruse became a detriment. Due to later political maneuverings and tradeoffs, it never became necessary to reveal Drake's claim for England, although in many later diplomatic confrontations concerning claim for northwest North America, England always referred back to Francis Drake's voyage.

Drake left a legacy for North America's generations of the future. His indisputable land claim has been the key to revealing that North America has a false history for the period between 1492 and the middle 1800s. This historical mix up was caused by the original Spanish latitude deception. The false documentation became so prevalent in world libraries that it was never possible to correct it. Modern communication now creates an opportunity to rework the old fake documentation and set forth the truth.

Queen Elizabeth I Knighting Drake

PHOTO SECTION

Donald M. Viles at six years old, with Sister Arline Viles at three years old. Taken in Portland, Oregon at Northwest 18th & Glisan Streets in 1927.

**Freshman Class at Newport High School 1935.
Donald M. Viles was fourteen years old.**

Back row – W. Bear, H. Guthrie, C. Pond, K. Baird, M. Gray.
Second row – K. Daywait, B. McKevitt, N. Johnson, **D. Viles**, V. Howard, L. Harris.
Third row – E. Smith, B. Fogarty, Z. Dickson, M. Andersen, C. Wait, M. Gilliland, E. Rowlands, R. Church.
Fourth row – V. Stocker, R. Pritchett, H. McKenzie, G. Johnson, D. Sumner, P. Smith, G. Price
Fifth Row – A. Rodli, M. Thurrell, W. Cobbs, S. Allphin, B. Sheppard, P. Martin.

Both photos from the Lincoln County Historical Society archives.

Newport High School in 1935.

A self-portrait by Donald M. Viles at Lava Lake, Canada, seventy miles north of Terrace, British Columbia.

Francis Drake In The New World 149

Charlene Viles taken in British Columbia, Canada while doing research. Photo by Donald M. Viles.

Donald M. Viles (facing camera) unloading a fishing boat. The fish was for "101 Seafoods," the fishing plant he built and owned in Garibaldi, Oregon. Photo taken in 1954.

About The Author

My father, Donald Marion Viles, was born on October 1, 1921 in Juneau, Alaska. He passed away at his home in Garibaldi, Oregon on October 25, 1995.

Don's mother was Hallie Arline Boone. Hallie's grandfather was George Luther Boone. George was a great-grandson of frontiersman Daniel Boone, one of the first folk heroes of the United States. George and his wife, Mourning Ann Young, had built a house on Yaquina Bay at what is now known as Boone's Point on the Bay Road between Newport and Toledo, Oregon.

George and Mourning Ann had fourteen children, one of whom was William Clay Boone. William married Marie Lindsley Baldwin and they built their house across the field from William's parents. That house is where Don's mother, Hallie, was born and the house still stands today. As a young woman, Hallie had a job interviewing the men who built the Yaquina Bay Bridge.

Don spent his childhood years in Juneau, Alaska and Portland, Oregon. After Hallie divorced Paul Viles, Don, his mother and his sister, Arline, moved to Newport, Oregon where Don attended high school until the age of fifteen. At that point, Don went to work in the woods as a logger to help support his mother, his sister and himself.

After logging for a number of years, Don turned to the ocean and became a commercial fisherman. He fished from California to Alaska and it was during this time that he became interested in the shipwrecks of the Pacific coast, navigation, geography and history.

In the early 1950s, Don and his wife Charlene built a business they named *101 Seafoods* in Garibaldi, Oregon. Later, he learned the printing trade and together with his wife, established a printing business. They named the print shop *Char-Don Printing,* also located in Garibaldi.

The picture above is of Don Viles and his printing press. It was taken a short time before Don retired in 1990. Don donated this printing press to the Tillamook County Pioneer Museum and it can still be seen in the front window of the *Headlight Herald* in Tillamook, Oregon. Don also worked for a number of years as a freelance reporter for the Portland *Oregonian* newspaper and wrote several articles for *Lost Treasure* magazine.

—Donna Viles Sheldon

INDEX

Alaska, 119, 125, 143
Angel, 46, 48, 49, 53
Arctic Ocean, 14, 117, 125
Argonaut, 121
arquebus, 75, 85, 91, 103
Augur Rock, 130-133, 135, 138, 141
Baia de los Fuegos, 119
Baja de los Fuegos, 120
Balboa, Vasco Nunez de, 98
Baldwin, Marie Lindsley, 150
Barncardo, 82
Barranquilla, 90
Bay of Fire, 116
Bear, 105, 147
beeswax, 14, 128
Bering Sea, 116, 125, 143
Bering Strait, 118
Bodega Bay, 118
Boone, Daniel, 150
Boone, George Luther, 150
Boone, Hallie Arline, 150
Boone, Mourning Ann Young, 150
Boone, William Clay, 150
Boone's Point, 150
Bourne, William, 137-141
Buckland Abbey, 17, 18
Cabecas Rocks, 108
Cabrillo, Juan, 60, 119, 143
Calvin, John, 29
Camden, 19
Canada, ix, 117, 148
Caribbean, 37, 38, 40, 47, 59, 61, 73, 81, 82, 97, 105
Cartagena, 49, 81-83, 85, 86, 90, 91, 106
Castellanos, Miguel de, 40, 41, 48, 49, 65

Castle Church of Wittenberg, 29
Cathwas Bay, 88
Chagres River, 80, 96, 100, 107
Char-Don Printing, 151
Charles V, 29
Chief Pedro, 97, 99, 100
Cimarrones, 68, 71-73, 75, 80, 89, 95, 97, 99, 103, 107-109
Coast Pilot, 115
Colima, 116
Colnett, James, 115, 120, 121
Colon Bay, 107
Columbus, Christopher, 28, 35, 63
Cook, Captain James, 115
Cook's Inlet, 125
Cordillera de San Blas, 97
Cortez, Hernan, 121
Cotton, Sir Thomas, 22
Crowndale Farm, 18-20
Darian coast, 64, 70, 86, 87
Devil's Cove, 119
Digges, Leonard, 136
Dragon, 60-63
Drake, Edmund, 18-23, 26
Drake, John, 19, 80, 86, 89, 90, 94
Drake, Joseph, 95
Drake's Bay, 118-120
Duke of Alva, 55, 58
Fairway Rock, 118
Fisher Research Laboratories, 133
Fletcher, Francis, 139
Fort Diego, 89, 90, 93
Frobisher, Martin, 139, 142

INDEX (CONTINUED)

fumeroles, 120
Gamboa, 96
Garibaldi, 149-151
Garrett, John, 67, 70, 89
Gilbert, Humphrey, 142
Gillingham Reach, 22
glyphs, 15, 132, 135
Golden Hinde, 14, 113-114,
   116-118, 120, 124, 125
Golfo de Morrosquillo, 91
Golfo de San Blas, 88
Grace of God, 47, 53
Hakluyt Society, 14
Hallo Bay, 119
Hawkins, John, 34, 37-40, 42,
   46-48, 50, 51, 53, 54, 56,
   58, 59
Hawkins, William, 22, 32
Hilliard, 17, 18
Hixom, Ellis, 80
Hondius Broadside, 120
Horsey, Sir Edward, 68
Isla de Tierra Bomba, 85
Island of California, 121-123
Isle of Bastimentos, 76, 78
Isles of Pines, 70, 73, 79, 80
Isthmus of Panama, 61, 65,
   79, 87, 95-102
Jensen, Wayne, Jr., 127, 128
Jesus of Lubeck, 46-51, 53
Judith, 46-55
Jungling, Emilee Boone, x
Jungling, Terence Boone,
   viii, x
King Philip, 32, 38, 39, 41,
   44, 46, 47, 48, 65, 85, 95
Land of Ten Thousand
   Smokes, 119, 120
Le Testu, 106, 107, 109, 110
Lion, 70
Lovell, John, 39, 40
Luxan, Don Francisco de, 52
Magdalena River, 90, 92
Magellan, Ferdinand, 13, 63

Mandinga, 88
Manila Galleon, 15
Martin Luther, 29
Medley, 31
Minion, 46, 51, 53, 54, 70,
   105, 106
Moluccas Islands, 80
Moone, Thomas, 87
Nass River, 124
Neah-Kah-Nie, 15, 127, 129,
   135-141
Newman, Mary, 57
Nombre de Dios, 65, 70, 72,
   74, 76, 77, 79, 81, 83, 84,
   86, 88, 90, 95, 100, 101,
   106-108, 110
Nootka, 120
Nunivak, 125
Nuttall, Zelia, 14
Oxenham, John, 98, 106, 108
Pasha, 64, 66-67, 88
Pelican, 114
Perivil of Hull, 89
Philip II, 29
Philippine Islands, 14
Pie, 132, 133
Pike, Robert, 102
Pillar of Hercules, 118
Plymouth, 17, 21, 31, 53-55,
   57, 60, 64, 67
Pope Alexander, 34
Port of Colon, 96
Port Pheasant, 66-70, 89
Portland Inlet, 124
Prince Henry of Portugal, 62
Puerto Escribanas, 97
Queen Elizabeth I, 14, 29,
   41-47, 51, 55-59, 62, 63,
   81, 82, 91, 114-117, 121,
   130, 138, 142
Ranse, James, 68-73, 79- 81
Reformation, 17, 29, 58
Rio de la Hacha, 40, 48, 65,
   79, 92

INDEX (CONTINUED)

Rio del Tizon, 123-124
Rio Francisco, 108
River of Firebrands, 116, 123
San Blas Bay, 97, 108
San Domingo, 84
San Juan de Ulloa, 49, 50,
    52-58, 65, 68, 79
Santa Marta, 92
Seville, 84, 85
Sheldon, Donna Viles, 7, 151
Short Sands Beach, 141
Silva, Ambassador de, 44,
    46, 47
Smith, Pat, 130
Spanish Armada, 13, 60
Spanish Inquisition, 29
Spes, Don Guerau de, 55, 56
St. Nicholas Island, 21, 22
Strait of Anian, 60, 116-118
Strait of Juan de Fuca, 14,
    118
Stuart, Mary, Queen of
    Scots, 58
Swallow, 46, 53
Swan, 60-67, 86-89
Tavistock, 18, 21
territory claim, 130, 136, 137,
    142
Tillamook County Pioneer
    Museum, 138
Tiny Island, 120
Tizons, 124
Tolu, 91
treasure, viii, ix, 18, 50-51,
    59, 65, 69, 75-81, 85, 89,
    90, 95, 96, 99, 100, 102,
    106-109, 114, 128, 130,
    138, 139, 141
Treasure Rocks, 15, 128-133,
    138
triangulation, 129-133, 136-
    141
Vancouver, George, 115
vara, 133, 134
Vara, Valencia, 137
Venta Cruces, 96, 99-103,
    105, 107
Venta Cruz, 80
Vera Cruz, 49, 61, 62
Veragua, 106
Viles, Arline, 146, 150
Viles, Charlene, 6, 113, 149
Viles, Paul, 150
Wagner, Henry, 113
Wayne's Rock, 133, 135
Wendle's Rock, 133-135,
    138, 141
William and John, 46, 53, 68
Yaquina Bay, 150
Zeeland, 47